Gathered Beneath the Storm

Gathered Beneath the Storm

Wallace Stevens, Nature and Community

JUSTIN QUINN

UNIVERSITY COLLEGE DUBLIN PRESS
PREAS CHOLÁISTE OLLSCOILE
BHAILE ÁTHA CLIATH

FIRST PUBLISHED 2002 BY UNIVERSITY COLLEGE DUBLIN PRESS,
Newman House, 86 St Stephen's Green, Dublin 2, Ireland
www.ucdpress.ie

ISBN 1 900621 66 5 (hardcover)
ISBN 1 900621 67 3 (paperback)

Cataloguing in Publication data available from the British Library

Designed by Lyn Davies
Typeset in Ireland in 10/12.5 Minion
by Elaine Shiels, Bantry, Co. Cork
Printed in Great Britain by MPG Books Ltd, Bodmin, Cornwall

Contents

Acknowledgements

Writing a book on Wallace Stevens and the nexus in his poetry between ideology and nature outside America has been a strange experience. In Ireland, where I began it, he is seldom read, and in the Czech Republic, my adopted home, barely heard of. On the one hand, there are certain disadvantages to this: first, the work is outside the pale of most critical debate, and thus there are few people to talk to about it; second, the landscapes and ideologies of Europe are very different from those of America, so that one constantly has to correct one's apprehensions of both when reading the poetry – there is a kind of delay between what Stevens says about society and nature and how one thinks of one's own environment. But there are advantages also, not least that one approaches the poet out of a different critical context, and thus, hopefully, is vouchsafed different insights into the poetry.

On a more practical level, it would have been much more difficult to write this book outside America without the help and encouragement of the following individuals who read and commented on drafts over the last few years: Ron Callan, Bonnie Costello, Thomas Docherty, Alan Filreis, J. C. C. Mays, David Wheatley, and Andrew Zawacki. In 1997 and 2000 I held courses on the poet at the Charles University, Prague, and the excellent students who participated made me think again about Stevens. The Department of English at Trinity College, Dublin, provided financial assistance during the initial stages of research; the Department of English and American Studies at the Charles University allowed me valuable time off towards the end of work on the book, for which I am also grateful. Provision of a generous grant to spend five months in the US was made by Fulbright Commission in Prague. The Department of English at Boston University, and especially Bonnie Costello who hosted my stay, provided a haven of libraries and stimulating conversation. The staff at the Huntington Library in San Marino were of great help. And for their warm welcome during that stay I'd like to thank Jana and Robert Kiely, and the Oliver, Menton and Corcoran families. Thanks also go to both my parents, Jack and Anna Quinn, and parents-in-law, Jan and Zdeňka Líman, without whose different kinds of generosity I could not have begun and completed this work.

Stephen Matterson, encouraged me from the start and kept a keen eye on the many metamorphoses the work underwent. Without the sharp intellectual attention which he devoted to the reading of endless drafts, the book would be many times poorer. He gave support when blind alleys swung into view, and criticised when there was need. My thanks to him are great. The shortcomings of the book remain, of course, my own. And finally I wish to thank my wife, Tereza Límanová, whose help, questions and conversation transformed and enlarged my perspective in many ways during the course of this work. I thank her for this and for much more.

My gratitude to Michael Schmidt of *PN Review*, John Serio of the *Wallace Stevens Journal* and Martin Procházka of *Litteraria Pragensia*, where parts of this book have already appeared, and especially to the many anonymous readers of the second. All quotations in this book are used for critical purposes only, and the words quoted remain the property of the individual copyright holders. A critical study like this necessarily has a dependent relationship on the *Collected Poems* of Wallace Stevens and my presumption is that readers will have a copy of this book close to hand; the page references I give are to both the Knopf and Faber editions.

JUSTIN QUINN
Charles University, Prague
August 2001

Abbreviations

CP Wallace Stevens, *The Collected Poems of Wallace Stevens*, New York: Knopf, 1991.

L   Holly Stevens, ed., *Letters of Wallace Stevens*, Berkeley: U of California P, 1996.

NA Wallace Stevens. *The Necessary Angel: Essays on Reality and the Imagination*, London: Faber & Faber, 1984.

OP Milton J. Bates, ed., *Opus Posthumous*, Revd ed. New York: Vintage Books, 1990.

SP Holly Stevens, *Souvenirs and Prophecies: The Young Wallace Stevens*, New York: Knopf, 1977.

Introduction

Much criticism of American poetry today can be split into two camps: that which is concerned with political and ideological contexts and that which is not. The division is not new, but with the rise of movements like New Historicism and the issues of identity politics spreading through the academy, the books and articles being written have a distinctly new character. Spearheaded by scholars whose main interests are not exegesis and appreciation of literary texts, these movements have had the effect of pushing the best readers of literature into unhelpful rearguard actions.[1] Perhaps most pernicious of all is polarisation: after all, why shouldn't there be a criticism which attends to the societal contexts of poetry without reneging on responsibilities to poetry as a discourse distinct from politics and ideology, one with its own special rhetorical funds and resources, which can nevertheless allow it to comment on the political aspects of our lives in special ways? Why shouldn't there be a criticism of literature that is not in thrall to the reductive narratives of leftist thought (praising the ideologically sound, contemning the rest) and is open to other ideological configurations, bourgeois or otherwise? The great strength of Marxist criticism lies in its descriptive powers; it is weaker in its value judgements. Why shouldn't criticism make use of those powers of description without the moralising that so often accompanies them?

Of course, the call for such criticism is not new either. It was made most memorably perhaps by Alfred Kazin in *On Native Grounds* in 1942:

> It may be sufficient to say that I have never been able to understand why the study of literature in relation to society should be divorced from a full devotion to what literature is in itself, or why those who seek to analyze literary texts should cut off the act of writing from its irreducible sources in the life of men. (x)

It appears that a younger generation of critics, brought up on deconstruction and feminism, is beginning feel this need once again. Tired of the old descriptions of the world, ideological and non-ideological, they are writing books which span this divide and renew our sense of the particularly literary aspects of poems, while also attending to political contexts and the ways in which poetry matters to lives. It is my hope that this study of Stevens belongs to this approach. In it, I offer readings of his poetry that show how the space of nature, far from allowing him to escape societal concerns, was the greatest occasion for his engagement of them. When he wants to think about politics and ideology, time after time he turns to the space of nature and lets these issues take on form there in order to meditate on them. Thus, to think about Leninism, he places Lenin on a park bench and observes the ideological arrangements of natural space that ensue. And thus to think in general about how ideologies change lives he observes a bouquet and its surroundings, the premise being that ideology, if it is to take purchase on reality, must transform the space of immediate human perception.

I should say here that the political and ideological aspects of the poetry I draw attention to in my discussion of Stevens's use of nature are very different from what we find in Kazin. Stevens does not think about ideology or political eras in the same way as, say, John Dos Passos. He does not write about society in terms of the stories of different people that make it up but rather at a secondary, theoretical level of experience. Stevens is concerned with the *ground* of the political, and following from this, he is concerned with its mechanisms, and how ideological change is necessarily a change in the way society views the individual, the collective and their relations. For instance, in Benedict Anderson's evocative phrase, a nation is an 'imagined community'; leaving aside the contemporary emphasis on its 'constructedness' and, what supposedly follows from this, its lack of validity, Stevens is preoccupied with the ways in which such imagining of the community takes place. His work, on a thematic level, moves in almost the same sphere of discourse as theory, vouchsafing the same kind of panoramic vision as Anderson and others, but it does so not through philosophical prose, but by employing the rhetorical resources and powers available to poetry. His general statements are arrived at through parable, example and persona; he constantly readjusts his course with fillips of humour and exclamation; and most important of all he conveys 'the great interests of man: air and light, the joy of having a body, the voluptuousness of looking' (CP 136).

Connected with this, he is concerned with how aesthetic space is imbricated in the space of political praxis. For instance, a common figure for the arrangements of the aesthetic is a vase of flowers in a room. In a poem like 'The Bouquet', as I read it in the first chapter, our perception of this object is conditioned by the house that frames it and more largely the land and nation beyond. For him, ideology is *readable* in the immediate world of perception and private desire. This is not political poetry as we commonly know it, but to deny it the title is to impoverish our own imaginative resources for thinking about communities and our place in them.

As has been pointed out so ably by Melita Schaum in her *Wallace Stevens and the Critical Schools* (1988), Stevens's poetry has been one of the sites of contest for various transformations in critical theory in the United States. The most significant recent trend in Stevens criticism has been historicist, and while these critics have told us important things about the contemporaneous contexts of Stevens's poetry, we are left wondering at the end if it has any relation to our own moment. I would hope that my approach that shows the unique way in which Stevens thinks about politics and ideology through the space of nature has implications not only for how we read the generations of poets which were influenced by him, but also as to how we think about how communities imagine themselves, whether against the space of nature, or as Rob Wilson contends, against a stranger postmodern sublime (206).

I do not discuss Stevens's career chronologically, but thematically. Thus in the readings that follow I will often juxtapose early with late poems, pointing out their similarities or dissimilarities when dealing with certain locales, tropes or occasions. Of course, Stevens's poetry did change throughout his life and I remark upon certain shifts (for instance his move from considerations of the masses in the 1930s and early 1940s to a stronger interest in community in the last phase); but in general what I find of more interest is the consistency of preoccupations and of ways of thinking over the long course of his career.

In Chapter One, I address the ways in which Stevens sings exaltations of the individual imagination in the midst of nature and places these against political and societal backdrops, exploring the implications of the visions of the Romantic mind for its community. In Chapter Two, I compare Stevens with one of the most strident and vocal American nature poets of the twentieth century, Robinson Jeffers. For the latter, nature was the fuel for his misanthropic rhetoric, its most attractive quality being that, whatever nature was, it was not made by humanity. Whereas Jeffers's nature is indentured to a particular ideology, Stevens refuses to employ its images in the service of any particular agenda; rather, in his poetry we see how nature is the site where the constructions of human agency – be they polities or aesthetics – are interrogated, or undone, or sometimes even validated. For Stevens, these constructs must be somehow answerable to the moments of exaltation we experience in nature. The pleasures of the open air, the sky, the land stretching off into the distance – these are things that were the hypostases of his thought. This comes through particularly clearly in a letter to Hi Simons:

> The 'ever jubilant weather' is not a symbol. We are physical beings in a physical world; the weather is one of things that we enjoy, one of the unphilosophical realities. (L 348–9)

It is this joy in the panoramas of nature that informs all of his poetry; but at no point does he exclude the political or the ideological in order to enhance his picturesque scenes. That is the falsification of the romantic: rather his thought follows the multiplicate filaments that link such awarenesses to the configurations of the political and ideological.

3

In Chapter Three, I will show how Stevens faces such 'falsifications of the romantic' directly. I open with a discussion of recent criticism of Romanticism which sees in the Romantic turn toward nature a repression of history. Imperial landscape, as W. J. T. Mitchell argues, excludes all elements that would conflict with its ideology ('Imperial Landscape' passim). Stevens's poetry, on the contrary, valorises the figure who is able to abandon this type of 'imperial' enclosure and face the open horizon of nature with all its hermeneutic uncertainty. (Here I will compare Stevens with Frost, a poet for whom the open–enclosed opposition was also significant.) The reading of the important late poem, 'The Auroras of Autumn', will figure all of these issues. There Stevens does indeed reserve his approbation for the figure who abandons his house to face the auroras; nevertheless, I argue that this in no way implies that Stevens relinquishes fictions. The enclosures humanity constructs around itself (political, religious, aesthetic) must be intermittently abandoned and destroyed so that new ones may take their place. Those new ones must be constructed by figures of capable imagination, in other words, those whose constructs are answerable both to their communities and to the horizons of nature. My characterisation here is very close to the previous critical talk of Stevens and fictions, but I wish to stress the communal nature of these negotiations: for Stevens it is the phases of the relations between society and nature, not just of some Emersonian transparent eyeball, that concern him.

Chapter Four will consider the human configuration of the city and its role in the poetry. Romantic writers often opposed their visions of nature with negative images of the city: Emerson, for instance, holds that transcendental truth can only be obtained by abandoning cities and going out into the midst of nature. Stevens is usually situated firmly in this tradition (i.e., by Bloom, Lentricchia and Hertz, among others). My reading, however, will show a Stevens who refuses this reductive opposition and seeks a visionary balance between the city and nature, which is in turn connected with his refusal of those ideologies which would restrict our apprehension of the many selves and sensuous worlds that populate the air, as the poem 'Esthétique du Mal' has it.

Chapter Five will be concerned firstly with the connections between family and nature, and then expand to consider the role of nationality, of landsmen and strangers. The figure that abandons enclosures is quite often an émigré. For instance, in 'Our Stars Come from Ireland' Stevens argues that by leaving the nation of your birth you leave a self behind, and once in your adopted country you have to invent a new self to face the new land. This is in line with his favouring of aliens over indigenes (who have become too ensconced in the enclosures discussed in Chapter Two). However, having argued so far that nature in Stevens's poetry is unideological, here I will discuss the idea that there is one major exclusion from the landscapes – that which is made on the basis of race.

Underlying this argument, as I have pointed out above, is the conviction that Stevens is still thinking about the role the political plays in our lives even when he is most pastoral. Thus, for me the poetry of the final phase of his career

(*Transport to Summer*, *The Auroras of Autumn*, and *The Rock*) does not abandon such issues, but rather sounds them more deeply. This is what has been missed in recent readings of Stevens by James Longenbach, Steven Miskinis, and Alan Filreis that locate him in relation to politics: Stevens needs a *space* to think about history and politics, and that space is nature and its objects; it is the Romantic unfalsified, the exaltations of the soul beneath the jubilant sky, exaltations that do not exclude all thought of the city with its masses of humanity spread out in irregular grids, and that space allows us to think about those very matters more clearly and more strangely.

Chapter 1

Wild flowers

1

On 20 September 1939, Wallace Stevens wrote a curious letter to Leonard C. van Geyzel in Ceylon (L 342–3). In the first paragraph he thanks van Geyzel for his gift of some translations of poetry from the Sinhalese. The next paragraph abruptly introduces two new subjects to the letter: the first, cursorily, is the outbreak of the war, and the second is peculiar English-influenced architecture of one part of Virginia, where Stevens was staying at the time. He expatiates on the second at length, prompting one to wonder if the apparent apathy with which Stevens refers to the outbreak of World War II perplexed his correspondent in Ceylon. It seems strange that such an important event as this would make no impact on the poet and would serve only as a temporal marker for his distinctions and *aperçus* relating to the houses and landscape of Virginia, where he spent part of the summer. What could the fact that the people there, as Stevens states, 'have some sense of style about living' have to do with the announcement of war? Is Stevens oblivious to the disasters and transformations of international politics, and above all to the fact that large numbers of people will die and many more suffer? The direction of Stevens's thought in this passage seems to confirm the characterisation of him by the New Critics as uninterested in anything beyond aesthetics.

However, the letter continues:

As the news of the development of the war comes in, I feel a horror of it: a horror of the fact that such a thing could occur. The country is more or less divided between those who think that we should hold aloof and those who think that, at the very least, we ought to help the British and the French. Our sympathies are strongly with the British and the French, but this time there is an immensely strong feeling about staying out. (L 342)

Although the drift is towards US non-involvement, Stevens expresses his 'horror of the fact that such a thing could occur' and also, further on, the hope that the events will not affect his correspondent (for an excellent account of Stevens's changing attitude to World War II see Filreis [*Actual World* 3–28]). Just when it seemed that he was satisfied to wander off into purely aesthetic realms, it turns out that all along he was thinking of the terrible prospect of the impending war. Arguably, there is even a connection made between the landscape of Virginia and his summary of opinions on the war in the US: as James Longenbach points out, that part of the American landscape is clearly English serves as a reminder of America's debts to England, in everything from laws to landscape art (209).

Bracketed as they are by World War II, his descriptions of Virginia present 'a complex of emotions' (CP 377). There is, on the immediate level, a desire on Stevens's part to convey something of the feel of a particular American place to his distant correspondent (something that he required in turn of van Geyzel, and Stevens's poetry as a result makes occasional reference to Ceylon). But going beyond this, there is also a desire to locate the horrific news in a particular locale, to provide his correspondent with a sense of what the news means in America as opposed to Paris or Ceylon. The fields of Virginia will probably remain oblivious and prosperous whatever happens in Europe; a Londoner's 'complex of emotions' when hearing the news must inevitably be very different, as must an Alsatian's, a Czech's or a Ceylon expatriate's. So, as he continues, we realise that World War II does not provide a backdrop for his consideration of the Virginia landscape, rather the relationship is more complex. What at first seemed like the indulgence of a poet in his ivory tower turns out to be a nuanced account of the different effects the war will have in different parts of the world.

In this book I argue that in his poetry Wallace Stevens uses landscape and natural objects in general as the occasions for thinking about politics and ideology. Previous generations of readers – New Critical, Post-Structuralist, New Historicist – have failed to recognise that in Stevens's poetry the pastoral setting is the space in which he meditates most intensely on the way that human societies produce cultural and political meaning, and not a respite from those pressures. Just as in the letter to Ceylon the reader must often go by indirection to witness Stevens thinking politically, so too in the poetry. A wide open horizon can be the locale for this work of the imagination and equally a flower in a vase, the flower working as synecdoche for landscape and nature in general. In both cases, it is objects shaped by the plastic force of nature that provide Stevens with the means to think about human arrangements of houses and ideologies. It is as though the intricate structures of nature *interrogate* those of man. After all, humanity only rearranges and recombines materials taken from the land, for the purposes of shelter or nutrition, practical or spiritual. And Stevens's sense of these activities – building a house, constructing a state, painting a landscape, farming a piece of land – as carried out by communities of people is acute. Groups of human beings have to arrange themselves under the huge expanses of the sky if they are not to be physically or spiritually engulfed, as poor Pip in *Moby-Dick*. And in all of these constructions – from the still life to the Capitol building – an ideology is implicit, a set of shared assumptions about the way that society should comport itself: these inform the central matter of style. As he thinks about the space of nature, with its lakes and mountains and flowerings, he is also aware that this is the space of ideology. I shall sketch out this connection later in reading 'The Bouquet', but to a large extent it is this particular Stevensian pastoral space that is the subject of the whole book.

For many years, his poetry had the reputation of being about the relation between Reality and the Imagination: the individual's creating mind (Imagination) faces a world of objects (Reality) and meditates on the relations between them. Sometimes the Imagination is in the ascendant, sometimes Reality. Such philosophical arguments couldn't seem further away from the space of political praxis. Nevertheless, in recent years there has been a movement in Stevens criticism to put him back, in Alan Filreis's phrase, in the actual world. Seminal to this movement has been Peter Brazeau's oral biography (1985). Its three-hundred-odd pages of interviews with Stevens's acquaintances, friends and business colleagues presented a view of the poet that helped critics revise old readings of the poems and see how the poetry was informed by the actual world all along.

These revisions have taken various forms. In the same year as Brazeau's biography, Milton J. Bates published his *Wallace Stevens: A Mythology of Self.* Drawing on material that would later appear in his revised edition of *Opus Posthumous* (1989), and with an enviable insight into the connections between Stevens's biography and his poetry, he re-read the poems for us revealing how the imaginative life of the poet was encrypted in them. As a general fact about poetry, this should hardly surprise us: after all, we expect that poetry is, to an extent, the story of a particular imagination's engagement with the world. However, in the case of Stevens, Bates's book was exhilarating news. Alerted to the fact that Stevens's life animated his poetry, that, say, his vacillation over the choice of a career, his personal reactions to World War I, impinged on his imaginative life sent many readers and critics back to the poems. There they encountered a Stevens who, for example, often wrote about war and who was not above addressing part of one long poem to a Marxist critic who had reviewed *Ideas of Order.*

Book after book presented us with yet another revision of Stevens. 1985 also saw the publication of Charles Berger's *Forms of Farewell: The Late Poetry of Wallace Stevens* in which, among other things, he presented a reading of 'The Auroras of Autumn' that suggested that its scope and ambition were fuelled by the trauma of nuclear war. The same year Albert Gelpi collected a group of essays by critics who had not heretofore written much on Stevens, *Wallace Stevens: The Poetics of Modernism*, including a wide range of approaches and attitudes to his work, from Marjorie Perloff's hostile essay indicting Stevens for ignoring history to Charles Altieri's praise of him as an exemplary poet of the political imagination. This essay adumbrated his magisterial *Painterly Abstraction in Modernist American Poetry* published four years later, a book that read the Romantic tradition in philosophical and ideological terms, and led to a consideration of Stevens at the apex of that tradition. It differed from most ideological critiques in that it was not Leftist and saw in Modernism exemplary political positions that remain important for readers today.

Helen Vendler's study of some of the shorter poems, *Words Chosen Out of Desire* (1986), countered the popular view of Stevens as an impersonal poet. She read the poems for the moments of revelation of personal pain and eros to which so many critics had remained deaf. Yet again we were presented with an 'actual' Stevens, connected on this occasion with the life of the emotions, unafraid to bring matters of personal loss and love into the poems. Frank Lentricchia, drawing on Bates's work, illuminated the poetry with respect to questions of gender-politics and the place of the male in Stevens's society. Underlying his investigations of the work of Michel Foucault and William James, and his readings of Stevens's poems, was the question of the place of the poet in the twentieth century. This was encapsulated in the title of his book, *Ariel and the Police* (1988).

The matter of Stevens's double life also fascinated Lentricchia, but it is perhaps the signal failing of Joan Richardson's two-volume biography of Wallace Stevens (1986, 1988) that there was barely any attention paid to his career in insurance. Richardson exhibited no sensitivity to the way the vicissitudes of this business, like any other, can engross the passions and intelligence of imaginative human beings. The insurance world was considered merely as something solid, a base that allowed Stevens to make his 'real' adventures in the writing of his poetry. Stevens's pre-eminence in the field of legal insurance and his dedication to that career indicate that his work at the Hartford was something more than a day job. Richardson's interest was purely in the literary and family backgrounds to his poetry. Another biography is waiting to be written that could take account of the daily metamorphosis that took place in Stevens's life, as he moved from poetry to business to poetry again.

And it is to the work of James Longenbach and Alan Filreis that we look for penetrating and exhaustive analyses of the nexus of Stevens's poems with the politics of the day. Without trying to foist political readings on poems that would plainly withstand them, their impressive scholarship placed Stevens's work in the context of contemporaneous politics and their sensitivity to the way that the poems give onto those politics provided a book that was illuminating for its account of the period and Stevens's imaginative involvement with it. The chapters in Longenbach's study, *Wallace Stevens: The Plain Sense of Things* (1991), dealing with 'Owl's Clover' and *Ideas of Order* are exemplary. Alan Filreis's *Wallace Stevens and the Actual World* came out the same year and concentrated on Stevens during the 1940s; three years later came his *Modernism from Right to Left: Wallace Stevens, the Thirties, and Literary Radicalism* that dealt with the preceding decade. Through extensive and painstaking archival research Filreis reconstructed the ebb and flow of Stevens's mind as he responded to newspapers, letters from friends, and economic and political change. Glen MacLeod's book, *Wallace Stevens and Modern Art* (1993), suggested interesting parallels between Stevens's poetic development and the contemporaneous developments in the New York art world. His scholarly research into the latter produced an interesting array of material that showed not only how Stevens's influenced some of the painters of the time, but also their effect on him from the Armory Show onwards. Stevens chatting in French with Marcel Duchamp at Walter Arensberg's apartment can stand as an image of just how close Stevens was to the revolutionary changes taking place in the art world of the twentieth century.

A healthy loosening of critical approach has occurred, which has served to enrich our sense of Stevens's work as poetry that addresses many issues beyond the purely metaphysical matters of Reality and the Imagination. However, excellent as some of these books are, I began this study out of a dissatisfaction with them. Yes, it's important to know about Stevens's relations with the art world and, yes, it's important to know how his biography informed his poetry, but each time I returned to the poems after reading one of these books I felt that much of the scope and subtlety of Stevens's engagements with that 'actual' world had been missed. The books by Filreis and Longenbach have, perhaps more than any others, changed the face of Stevens criticism in recent years. Exeunt the post-structuralist concerns of the 1970s and early 1980s, as represented by the work of J. Hillis Miller, Joseph Riddel, and Paul Bové; enter the actual world that Stevens lived in. To a great extent, my book quarrels with these critics: they go so far in imbricating Stevens's work in the political and cultural debates of the time that we are left wondering what use the poems can possibly be to us now. I contend that there is a mode of the political in Stevens's work, as revealed through his treatment of nature, and that by recognising this nexus in the poetry our view of Stevens's poems is changed. In a variety of voices and verse-forms, Stevens shows how the dramas and exaltations of the individual imagination abroad in nature or observing an object taken out of nature have a meaning beyond the arena of the transcending consciousness of the individual, that is in a public context: his poems propose that thinking in new ways about a bouquet or the landscape at Oley has a profound impact on the ways in which communities arrange themselves and think about their place in the world, which is, necessarily, the ground for thinking about politics.

The conviction that animates many of his poems is that any separation of these areas of thought is the evasion of a mind incapable of embracing imaginative complexity. Nature and landscape for Stevens are not of the Watteau variety, not sylvan idylls to salve our troubled minds. They are open to politics, to the contingencies of history, and the larger concerns of communities, precisely at the moment when they seem to abscond to pastoral. And although previous critics have discussed his involvement with his times, both in political and cultural terms, they have failed to trace the connections Stevens makes. By following these connections in the pages ahead, I wish to enlarge our ideas of the peculiar tracks Stevens leads us along, tracks that are of great interest to us now when the

11

relations between the categories of the aesthetic and the political are being debated so strenuously. I shall not engage these debates directly in this book, but would nevertheless like to think that by pursuing these particular paths in the poetry, I can show Stevens provided us with an air, a kind of music of the intellect, that is of much value to us when we confront basic questions of culture and politics in the present.

In its devalued state, such pastoral subject matter is considered 'aesthetic', in the pejorative sense of being separated from social and political concerns. The imagination flies the nets of government and country to a realm of aethereal beauty that has its own laws of proportion and balance. However, Stevens brings us back to the ideological valency of pastoral in a new way: it is just when he seems most abstracted in landscape that he is likely to make an abrupt turn and show the reader that there is a world outside the aesthetic object, or, more precisely, that if the aesthetic object is not to become etiolated and ultimately irrelevant it must constantly take cognisance of that world. To make a start at tracing some of these turns in the poetry, I want to go back to an older critical characterisation of Stevens that Frank Lentricchia deftly summarises, and which takes its main terms from Stevens's poetry and prose:

> Reality, as alien being, is a 'violence' which ever pressures us, as he put it in a well-known formulation, and the imagination is the response of our subjective violence which presses back against an inhuman chaos. Imagination makes space between us and chaos and thereby grants momentary release from sure engulfment, madness, and death. (*After the New Criticism* 33)

And then:

> Against an irrepressible will to identify the projections of desire, those 'longed-for lands,' with reality itself, he sets a critical self-consciousness which incessantly subverts and dismantles his fictions and shows them for what they are: 'intricate evasions of as.' (*After the New Criticism* 32)

This is the characterisation of the great heroic imagination, a description that engages much of the diction and turns of thought of Western philosophy from the Greeks on. By this account, Stevens's poetry is about the human mind facing an inimical world of objects that it must arrange and interpret, even though these arrangements and interpretations are provisional and will eventually fall apart. Figuring the imagination in terms of the demiurge facing primeval chaos and making something of it, this description of humans' 'fictionalising' takes its lead from Stevens's own statement, 'God and the imagination are one' (CP 524). However, it is a description that is more applicable to a work like Book II of *Paradise Lost* than Stevens's poetry: in the former, you have inhuman chaos, interminable voids, etc., whereas Stevens is more likely to have his figure of the capable imagination sitting in a park or looking at a bowl of flowers. And although Lentricchia presents Stevens's poetics in terms of the first-person plural in this passage, the prevailing figuration is that of the individual imagination heroically facing 'inhuman chaos': there is no sense of this imagination being part of a community, or of the invented fictions having a public meaning or of their occurring in public time. If only the inhuman chaos could be conjured up in a living-room, the whole affair could be safely conducted by the agonist from the comfort of his or her armchair.

What this characterisation misses is the way that Stevens is concerned with the public aspect of the imagination's tropes. Taking this further, he is often more interested in how the imagination of a particular community or nation works than in that of the individual. 'Sad Strains of a Gay Waltz' is about how collective emotion changes and creates new forms of music to answer new social conditions. He is, it is true, interested in how figures of capable imagination (say, the rabbi or the captain – both versions of the major man) can affect transformations in culture and society, but frequently their speech, which situates a community in the world, is part of a dialogue and not merely monologic preaching; moreover, the ultimate significance of their speech has less to do with the satisfactions it affords their own imaginations than with the 'true reconcilings' they provide the community (CP 144). Theirs is an art that takes cognisance of public emotion and thought at any particular moment and speaks in reaction to that, as reflection and redirection, and that the community recognise it as such is its ultimate justification for Stevens.

Following from this, we should note that such public figures do not work on the primeval void but more usually on human arrangements of landscapes, gardens or flowers in jars. The given is no inhuman chaos, rather it is a previous human construct that is no longer adequate to the needs of the imagination when trying to make sense of its world. Even when facing the sea – the closest earthly image we have of that 'inhuman chaos' – Stevens's figures encounter an element that has already found a place in human figurations many centuries ago. Observe Crispin crossing the Atlantic from Bordeaux (CP 28):

> Could Crispin stem verboseness in the sea,
> The old age of a watery realist,
> Triton, dissolved in shifting diaphanes
> Of blue and green?

As a later Stevens would have it: 'There was a myth before the myth began, / Venerable and articulate and complete' (CP 383); indeed, that the previous myth is so venerable, articulate and complete, is its main fault. In the case of this passage in 'The Comedian as the Letter C' the prior myth is that of Poseidon's son, who makes the roaring sound of the ocean by blowing through his shell, over which is laid the new picaresque myth of Crispin. Elsewhere it is a picturesque view of fields and hills, or the arrangement of a bouquet in a room that is the prior myth to be revised or reappraised; most often it is an object out of nature or nature itself, as, say, in 'The Auroras of Autumn'.

That landscape and more generally nature provide the most significant occasions for his rethinking of community and imagination raises several interesting points. First and foremost, nature is in so many respects traditionally seen as the fundamental basis for the values of a community, the source of its moral judgements about its members and the world. That an act or a thing is considered 'natural' or 'unnatural' is still used to establish whether it is 'right' or 'wrong'. Thus, when Stevens writes about nature, not as absolute origin that provides us with a moral code, but as the site of hermeneutic uncertainty and flux, as Bonnie Costello describes it, he is questioning the basis of social value and how it is produced ('Adequacy' 203–18). This he does in various ways, but I give just one example here: nationalist ideology has always moved swiftly to appropriate idealised representations of the landscape of its territory as validation of the national 'spirit'. The very words 'nation' and 'nature' are cognates. Visit any gallery in any country that has undergone a period of national awakening and there the dutiful pictures hang: mountains, sunsets, lakes, trees dramatically positioned against the sky; all scenes that justify a people's ownership of a particular terrain and, above all, its particular spirit. Quite a number of Stevens's poems explore and question these connections between 'nature' and 'nation', as I shall show in Chapter Five.

Nevertheless, Stevens recognises the human need for myths of origin and acknowledges that often nature is seen as the site of those myths, even while rejecting the notion that there can be a return to nature, that an unmediated relationship between a community and its particular landscape can be achieved. (Crispin does not face primeval chaos when crossing the Atlantic, but an ocean that had already been 'storied' by humanity.) This is the dilemma that many of his most important poems face. Nature appears as something that baulks human fictions and makes us aware of their constructedness. By considering a bouquet standing in the middle of the house, we realise that space is shaped in different ways by the flowers and the constructed walls. The phases of this difference are what Stevens often writes about.

Just as in his letter to van Geyzel where he employs the Virginia landscape to help him comprehend the news of the outbreak of war, so too he needs the horizon of nature to understand all of humankind's fictions, be they houses, paintings or nations. Moreover, for all his decreation of romantic correspondences he is acutely aware that it is in the midst of nature that humanity experiences its most exalted moments. A poem like 'The Auroras of Autumn' has him searching the skies for the forms of nobility that his figure of the 'major man' ultimately couldn't provide. The auroras are a force moving through the heavens, a kind of supreme fiction that changes, gives pleasure, and they are, like the sea, very close to a plastic representation of abstraction; they elicit from him his profoundest meditations on the relations between the individual imagination and the community. A natural phenomenon prompts these thoughts. However, this is so far from our conventional idea of nature poetry that it has never been recognised as such. And yet what are the auroras if not one of nature's grandest performances? Each bidding of farewell is a further decreation, but these cease halfway through the poem as Stevens shifts to wonderment in reaction to the manifestation of the natural world at its most untrammelled and festive moment.

In *Notations of the Wild: Ecology in the Poetry of Wallace Stevens* (1997), Gyorgyi Voros argues that this demonstrates that his poetry can be read as proto-deep-ecological that 'reimagines the Nature / culture dialectic and seeks to reinstate the forgotten term – Nature or, to use Stevens's term, 'reality' – in that dialectic' (11). While Voros makes her case with elegance and inventiveness, she simplifies the poems by seeing in them such a tendency to valorise Nature over humanity. There is no doubt that Stevens is much more occupied with Nature than most of his Modernist peers and in ways that have for many years been overlooked. (One exception to this is Bonnie Costello's 'Wallace Stevens: The Adequacy of Landscape', an article which Voros does not refer to in her book, and which I shall discuss in Chapter Two.) But he shares nothing of the deep ecologist's fear that Nature is near exhaustion. In this respect, his ideas of nature are closer to those of the nineteenth century than our world of global warming and depleted rain forests. Moreover, this approach supposes that Stevens was unaware that things like landscapes and the idea of wilderness itself were cultural constructs (as he so economically points out in 'Anecdote of a Jar'). Voros's reading is the same as the older characterisation, with the inimical 'inhuman chaos' replaced by a more compliant idea of 'Nature'. Her ecological approach gives a public significance to Stevens's poetry, but is anachronistic in the way it projects our concerns into the past.

His poems argue in different ways and to different ends: they show how our aesthetic thoughts about the landscape and objects from nature extend to the public realm of political praxis, or, in other words, when we are thinking about flowers we are also thinking politically, indeed that the flowers often force us to think in new ways about social configurations. It is this movement between the categories of the 'aesthetic' (that is, natural objects) and the 'political' which constitute the pivot of so many of his poems and makes it difficult for him to be claimed for ecological thought. In 'Prelude to Objects' (CP 195) he intones:

Poet, patting more nonsense foamed
From the sea, conceive for the courts
Of these academies, the diviner health
Disclosed in common forms.

The 'nonsense foamed / From the sea' belongs to the category of the 'aesthetic', and what the poet must do is give these a wider public meaning. It is Stevens's knowledge that meditations on the landscape or studies of pears, etc., must be brought to court in this way that informs many of his poems.

Even now critics often work on the assumption that if a poet writes about the weather, the timothy grass, etc., and is not ecological as Stevens isn't, then he or she must be an 'aesthete', in the pejorative sense of the word. With such a simplistic opposition it is impossible to comprehend the greater part of Stevens's poetry. In 'Imagination as Value', writing about the relations between the imagination and social contexts he presents us with a set of complex interactions between these two apparent poles:

> Of imaginative life as social form, let me distinguish at once between everyday living and the activity of cultural organization. A theater is a social form but it is also a cultural organization and it is not my purpose to discuss the imagination as an institution. Having in mind the extent to which the imagination pervades life, it seems curious that it does not pervade, or even create, social form more widely. It is an activity like seeing things or hearing things or any other sensory activity. Perhaps, if one collected instances of imaginative life as social form over a period of time, one might amass a prodigious number from among the customs of our lives. Our social attitudes, social distinctions and the insignia of social distinctions are instances. A ceremonious baptism, a ceremonious wedding, a ceremonious funeral are instances. [. . .] Costume is an instance of imaginative life as social form. At the same time it is an instance of the acceptance of something incessantly abnormal by reducing it to the normal. It cannot be said that life as we live it from day to day wears an imaginative as aspect. On the other hand, it can be said that the aspect of life as we live it from day to day conceals the imagination as social form. (OP 145–6)

I quote at length to convey how Stevens's thinking is alive to the subtle ways in which the imagination is present in social forms. Beneath this is the Shelleyan conviction that *poesis*, the act of making, is carried out by artists as well as politicians (viz., his statement just a few pages earlier that Communism 'exhibits imagination on its most momentous scale' [OP 143]). For Stevens, pastoral is the site for thinking about these ideas. Going back to 'The News and the Weather' (CP 264–65) from *Parts of a World* (1942), we see in the first section how he sets up the world of social forms, invoking the context of the nation with its ceremonies, industry and labour problems, only to show it interpenetrated by natural elements, here the sun. 'The blue sun [. . .] caught the flags and the picket-lines / Of people, round the auto-works: // His manner slickened them. He milled / In the rowdy serpentines'. Poetry like this is very clearly gesturing towards the poetry of the Left with its mentions of the auto-works and picket-lines, but it is equally clear that it is not a Leftist tract. The sun's entrance breaks up the usual dialectic thinking that is associated with workers, and brings ambiguity. Is he for or against? Is he sympathising with the lot of the working class or mocking it? Conservative or communist? The poem simply won't answer this type of reductive question.

The second part of the poem is almost purely pastoral. For some readers this move might seem escapist (absconding from the picket-lines and auto-workers for the luxurious contemplation of magnolias and the changing seasons); the 'poison' mentioned is more a balm for the mind wracked by the social problems of the first section, '[f]or the spirit left helpless by the intelligence'. But there is a deeper intelligence in Stevens's move, and one that isn't escapist either, a knowledge that the weather, implying the wider horizon of nature and the changing seasons, is necessary to our understanding of the news (the picket-lines, etc.). This is not a rejection of social concerns but the provision of a horizon for them. In the terms of 'Imagination as Value' this poem brings the imagination (the sun, and later the monologue of Section II) into contact with social forms (the colours of the US flag, parades, picket-lines and auto-workers). The greatest moments of vision and emotion for the spirit occur in nature, and we must learn to see the connections between the six distichs of the two sections, just as we must learn to connect those moments with social forms.

Public formations such as the courts and academies in 'Prelude to Objects', if they are to have any meaning at all, must be capable of comprehending the most ecstatic moments of our being. Emerson abroad in the countryside at the beginning of *Nature* (1836) had to slough off the ties of social responsibility before gaining access to sublime emotions. Whitman followed him, and, borne by expansive feelings of nationalism, discovered how to relate such sublimity to almost everything in the life of the United States in the nineteenth century. For Stevens, as for nearly all the significant writers of Modernism, such nationalism was not an option: it no longer found purchase as an explanation of contemporary life (for a brief but persuasive discussion of this transition period see Pearce 253–6). How, then, can one continue thinking in terms of nations, and communities in general, without losing sight of those private moments of expanded awareness, those spots of time by which we try to steer our lives because they seem a revelation of the central truths of existence? This torsion of transcendence versus a return to the earth (with its courts and academies) is one of the fundamental elements of Stevens's thought.

Moreover, the attitude to nature and the natural object that comes out of all this is fundamentally different from the Coleridgean approach. When discussing the imagination in Chapter XIII of *Biographia Literaria*, Coleridge writes:

It dissolves, diffuses, dissipates, in order to recreate: or where this process is rendered impossible, yet still at all events it struggles to idealize and to unify. It is essentially *vital*, even as all objects (as objects) are essentially *fixed and dead*. [last italics mine] (167)

It is safe to say that sentences like these have conditioned critical views of Stevens for decades as a philosophical poet in this vein. Frank Doggett, discussing Stevens's use of the term 'reality', writes:

> To be real is almost a quality in itself for reality is the truth of existence, a feeling of the verity of things. Since a trust in the reality of things and selves fills out the void that would otherwise exist without a belief in a transcendent ground of being, the word *reality* holds an unconscious store of feeling in Stevens' use of it. (27)

Doggett's 'void' and Coleridge's expanse of 'fixed and dead' objects, upon both of which the magisterial human imagination works, is at odds at a basic level with the readings of poems that I shall offer in this book. In 'The Rock' we see that 'things and selves' are not so easily validated, and that 'reality' for Stevens, in one of his most important lyrics, is itself grounded upon the troping force of nature. It is to this agency that he looks in order to find 'a cure of the ground / Or a cure of ourselves, that is equal to a cure // Of the ground' (CP 526) and not to some static and featureless Cartesian extension. In a more flippant earlier mood, referring directly to Coleridge's influential coinage, he put it thus:

> He called the hydrangeas purple. And they were.
> Not *fixed and deadly*, (like a curving line
> That merely makes a ring).
> It was a purple changeable to see.
> And so hydrangeas came to be. (OP 43; italics mine)

The outright echo of Coleridge's phrase 'fixed and dead' marks how differently Stevens thinks about nature. For him the latter possesses an agency which challenges that of men, and more generally that of communities whose imaginative constructions work to situate them in the world. Observing the phases of these encounters opens up the poetry in important ways and shows how Stevens was a nature poet of particularly original mark.

2

The erratic trajectory of 'The Bouquet' (CP 448–53) exemplifies that which in other poems remains more oblique. The poem moves between a considera-tion of the bouquet of flowers, the house and landscape surrounding it, and the larger space of the nation. It demonstrates that, even at this stage in his career, when at least one commentator has said that he had lost most interest in relating matters of the imagination to politics (Longenbach 279), these ideas were still immediate for him. The first part of the poem offers contradictory signals, as

Stevens confuses the categories of inside and outside: is the bouquet a part of the genteel world of drawing room and house, or does it stand as synecdoche of the natural world?

> Of medium nature, this farouche extreme
> Is a drop of lightning in an inner world [. . .]

The word 'farouche' itself encapsulates these confusions: French-sounding and recherché, it conjures up a dandyish, effete nineteenth-century atmosphere – the old category of the aesthetic in all its fragility and irrelevance. Above all, that atmosphere is an enclosed space, very much apart from the great outdoors that a poet like Whitman choired. But delving into the word's etymology we see that it comes from the Latin for 'out of doors', with the *OED* even noting a connection, albeit obscure, between it and the word 'forest'. This contrast between inside and outside is amplified in the second line which has the lightning of the open sky penetrating 'an inner world'. These are the terms the poem sets for its meditation on the community and the sphere of political, even military action: inner worlds and outer expanses. The lightning penetrating the inner world foreshadows the clumsy officer who will enter the house at the poem's end.

But the poem is also about seeing. It is about the complexities of perceiving a simple human arrangement of flowers in a vase on a table, and the way large intellectual powers can inhere in everyday scenes, the flowers not just being things, but a whole host of 'para-things' that are not the fictive projections of the human imagination, but are a revelation of what lies in experience itself. As Charles Altieri says in his eloquent discussion of this late phase Stevens's career: 'there are not worlds and interpretations, but worlds as interpreted in a variety of ways, each perhaps best articulated, not by descriptions, but by making manifest the energies involved' (*Painterly Abstraction* 347). And, still following Altieri, rather than leaving the door open for a relativism that defers the shared values of a community, such poems establish sites where communities of readers can test the interpretations of the world that structures their lives. To put it differently, how you see the bouquet depends on a whole range of beliefs you hold about the world. In the second part of the poem Stevens makes it clear that the bouquet takes on a different aspect if it is seen 'in a land // Without a god'. The poem then becomes the site in which the arrangement of para-things (with their attendant various interpretations of the world) reveals 'portents of our own powers as readers', to quote Altieri quoting Stevens (*Painterly Abstraction* 340).

To face reality is to face this range of interpretations and this brings an enlargement of our powers:

> One approaches, simply, the reality
> Of the other eye. One enters, entering home,
> The place of meta-men and para-things,
>
> And yet still men though meta-men, still things
> Though para-things; the meta-men for whom
> The world has turned to the several speeds of glass [. . .]

This kind of search for nobility in quotidian experience is what Altieri finds in Stevens's late work, where plain propoundings and straightforward descriptions of objects and events can suddenly taken on great power. For instance, in 'An Ordinary Evening in New Haven' each canto is not a further abstraction removing us from the reality of the Connecticut town but rather a necessary embellishment that allows us to see it all the more clearly. Those meta-men, Stevens tells us, are those who have a particular nobility. It is the nobility of perceiving well, seeing the bouquet in all its multiplicity and not as belonging to the etiolated category of the aesthetic but as 'para-thing'; the flowers not as 'choses of Provence', but as part of the commonal that calls forth intellectual and more importantly emotional allegiances. The 'emotion' here is not an imaginative projection; it is part of the bouquet, part of the fund of common experience, available for all.

And then the poem turns. The bouquet is an object taken out of nature that precipitates these meditations, not simply another domestic object. Although arranged by human hands and placed in a vase, the flowers have been shaped by the climate and various tropisms, springing up from the earth beneath the open sky. 'Not all objects are equal' (OP 188), Stevens states in the Adagia. Thus, since the flowers are special objects, it behoves Stevens to look to that for which they stand as synecdoche: nature itself.

> Through the door one sees on the lake that the white duck swims
> Away – and tells and tells the water tells
> Of the image spreading behind it in idea.
>
> The meta-men behold the idea as part
> Of the image, behold it with exactness through beads
> And dewy bearings of their light-locked beards.
>
> The green bouquet comes from the place of the duck.

The promise hidden in the word 'farouche' is kept: our attention is directed 'out of doors', to the origin of the bouquet itself. The 'inner world' of human arrangements is dependent on an outer expanse, that of the landscape. There the pattern of things and para-things is paralleled by the duck and the ripples that spread out in its wake. It is because the bouquet 'comes from the place of the duck', i.e., the landscape, the horizon of nature, it is able to engender such aggrandisements of the intellect and imagination, like the auroras earlier in the same collection. The bouquet, as 'drop of lightning' from an outer world, might only be, in Emily Dickinson's phrase, 'remotest consulate' of the elemental force of the northern lights (Dickinson 1045), but consulate it is as it forces revisions of the constructed spaces of humanity. To understand the arrangement of the bouquet in the room we need to attend to the landscape stretching out from the house; this dependency of human space and natural space is captured in the enjambment, 'at a window / Of the land'.

The third part of the poem begins by suggesting that such ideas are imaginative investments in the object, not discoveries: the bouquet 'is quirked // And queered by lavishings of [the meta-men's] will to see'; but this is retracted as Stevens proclaimed that it is not a distortion but 'A freedom revealed, a realization touched'. It is only through such 'meta-vision' that the quotidian is experienced; anything else is a distortion, a restriction, an enslavement. The freedom revealed by this 'drop of lightning' from the natural world might lead us to believe that the land and its flowering are some kind of origin. Stevens recognises this need in humanity for such fictions of origin, but he – for want of a better word – disperses them, in the passage beginning 'Perhaps these colours [. . .]'. There is no origin at all except that of the particular arrangement of the bouquet right before our eyes. There is no ultimate apprehension of a nature unmediated by interpretation: there is just this détente between the flowers as shaped by nature and then arranged by human hands.

Beginning this reading of 'The Bouquet' I mentioned the poem's erratic trajectory. Up to the fourth section, it follows a smooth course as the meditation expanded out from the object, revising and qualifying previous statements at a rather stately pace. The short final section abruptly breaks this rhythm. Now it seems that thoughts that were previously expressed with discrimination and nuance are coarsely bellowed:

A car drives up. A soldier, an officer,
Steps out. He rings and knocks. The door is not locked.
He enters the room and calls. No one is there.

He bumps the table. The bouquet falls on its side.
He walks through the house, looks round him and then leaves.
The bouquet has slopped over the edge and lies on the floor.

What preceded was Stevens near his best; what we get now is something like Hemingway near his worst. On the face of it, this passage seems to be awkwardly proclaiming that no matter how subtle our theories and fictions, they can still be obliterated by incursions from the real. The cycle never stops. We had thought, in Section Two, that we had taken cognisance of the real, but here this is dismissed. This is the kind of dismantling of fictions that Lentricchia talks of.

21

Or is it? To me, its violence is less clumsy didacticism than a trial and validation of all the preceding thought. In 'Notes Toward a Supreme Fiction', Stevens states that the 'final elegance' of thought is not consolation or sanctification 'but plainly to propound' (CP 389). That is, if our thought cannot brook such plain speech, cannot take cognisance of a quotidian that includes families, soldiers, war, then it is of no use to us. Rather than an account of the imagination vanquished by reality, this passage is the crucial test of all the meta-seeing in the poem. The reader must be able to perceive objects not only when they are static, enclosed, arranged, but when they become part of larger processes and horizons, part, even, of a different speech. If the poem has not taught us how to continue seeing the bouquet as para-thing through the events of the final section, then it has failed.

What is also of note is Stevens's indication that the man is not another visitor from Porlock, but part of a specific social formation: he is an army officer. Stevens reminds us that the space of political praxis, here particularly of martial action, is inextricably connected with all our previous thoughts about the bouquet. In Section Two he reminded us that our perception of the bouquet was dependent on the surrounding 'land', meaning the horizon of nature beyond the house; now it is 'land' as nation, in the figure of the officer, which impinges on our perception of the flowers. To refer again to 'Prelude to Objects', the diviner health must be disclosed in common forms. As we ponder the soldier further, we start to wonder why he has called to the house and why it is empty. Have its inhabitants fled before invading troops? Or has he returned from war unexpectedly to find his family absent? In either case, we suddenly become aware of the land in which the bouquet stands as being caught up in a larger international drama, just as in the letter to van Geyzel the Virginia landscape was – in Stevens's idea of it – part, however distant, of the outbreak of World War II.

It might be objected that this reading of the poem does not fit with my thesis about the connections between nature and politics in Stevens's poetry as the bouquet has little to do with the wild, open horizons of nature. It is just a particular arrangement of flowers, an object that could easily be replaced by a guitar, a bottle, a newspaper. This would be a fair comment if Stevens did not repeatedly bring the reader's attention to the fact that the bouquet has been taken out of nature and stands in the room as synecdoche of its wider backdrop. It is worth making this point here as similar situations – in 'The Bouquet' for example – occur through Stevens's poetry when he juxtaposes natural objects in still lifes with the spacious hinterland of nature beyond the frame of the painting or house. Thinking about the contiguities of nature and human arrangements forces him to think further about political arrangements of the world also. Take for instance 'The Countryman' (CP 429) where Stevens puns on the way a pastoral canto is sung in the political precinct of a canton. He attempts to face the quotidian matters of social structures (cities, polities) through '[a]n understanding beyond journalism' (OP 136), in other words without resorting to reductive accounts of life, nurturing the vision in which, as he says in 'The Bouquet', the world is seen through several speeds of glass. For Stevens, it is the objects of nature that sponsor this vision, a vision that comprehends the panoramas of politics and society as well as the individual imagination's most exalted moments of feeling.

3

I want to turn again to the letter to van Geyzel to draw attention to another aspect that is pertinent to many of his poems about nature and habitations; this is the connection he makes between the people, their houses and the style of the landscape. The connections to which he draws van Geyzel's attention make up the delicate fabric of what we can call 'place'. The English influence differentiates the area in Virginia where he found himself at the time from other places in the state. And while the English elements might be considered by some Americans as foreign, for Stevens the people of this place are natives in it since there is a continuity between the style of their lives, their houses and their land. In Chapter Five I shall look more closely at the idea of the natives and their lands in the poetry, but for now I wish to draw attention to the way in which Stevens, when faced with the idea of global war, needs the support of a particular place and a particular set of arrangements of objects in space to help him think through the looming disaster. Philosophical or political ideas only become sensible for Stevens insofar as he is able to think through them as a set of spatial relationships. In order to think about Nietzsche and Lenin in 'Description Without Place', rather than polemicising with statements from their writings he figures them in plastic situations: they sit before expanses of water, and their thought is characterised by how they represent that water to themselves. Compare such an approach with a contemporary poet's engagement with the German philosopher:

> [. . .] then we go back to the green-eyed heat, and stare,
> beating on the icy film between each thing, knocking, tapping,
>   to see what's happening,
> 'the wasteland grows; woe to him hiding wastelands
>   within' (The Portable
> Nietzsche – Viking '54 – we look in there) [. . .]   (Graham, The Errancy 55)

Rather than presenting us with the figure of Nietzsche himself Jorie Graham prefers quotation, providing us even with its provenance, which serves to make a physical connection (by giving her particular edition of Nietzsche) between the thought of the philosopher and the poet. Stevens is at once more impersonal and personal: the first because he establishes no autobiographical link as Graham does, the second because he thinks in terms of the philosopher's particular biography (CP 342):

> Nietzsche in Basel studied the deep pool
> Of these discolorations, mastering
>
> The moving and the moving of their forms
> In the much-mottled motion of blank time.

When referring to Lenin, the scene-setting is even more specific:

> Lenin on a bench beside a lake disturbed
> The swans. He was not the man for swans.
>
> The slouch of his body and his look were not
> In suavest keeping. The shoes, the clothes, the hat
>
> Suited the decadence of those silences,
> In which he sat. All chariots were drowned. The swans
>
> Moved on the buried water where they lay.
> Lenin took bread from his pocket, scattered it –
>
> The swans fled outward to remoter reaches,
> As if they knew of distant beaches; and were
>
> Dissolved. The distances of space and time
> Were one and swans far off were swans to come.
>
> The eye of Lenin kept the far-off shapes.
> His mind raised up, down-drowned, the chariots.
>
> And reaches, beaches, tomorrow's regions became
> One thinking of apocalyptic legions.

The chariots represent the feudal past that Lenin dispensed with, and the swans are at once the sign of an old aesthetic (they flee him much in the same way that writers like Nabokov, Khodasevich and Bunin did) and a future aesthetic that will reign after Lenin's day has come and gone (one thinks of White Russian writers published once again in their native country contributing to new developments in Russian literature). Arguably Graham's approach has a greater phenomeno-logical purity, bounded as it is by her own experience of Nietzsche, while Stevens must invent these images of political figures facing nature. But what I wish to draw attention to here is Stevens's insistence that ideology and politics are most clearly apprehended in this interview between man and nature. It is worth recalling the conclusion to 'Imagination as Value' in this context:

[T]o be able to see the portal of literature, that is to say: the portal of the imagination, as a scene of normal love and normal beauty is, of itself, a feat of great imagination. It is the vista a man sees, seated in the public garden of his native town, near by some effigy of a figure celebrated in the normal world, as he considers that the chief problems of any artist, as of any man, are the problems of the normal and that he needs, in order to solve them, everything that the imagination has to give. (NA 155–6)

Randall Jarrell remarked how Stevens was attracted by images of wilderness (138). This is a fair observation, but Stevens was also fascinated by the human boundaries placed on wilderness, thus his jar in Tennessee, and thus nature here arranged into a garden as the primordial site of poetry. The social connections Stevens asserts in the passage are significant: the poet-figure is in his *native* town; also, he cannot abscond from social configurations in his moment of transcedence because his awareness of the statue, which connotes the moral and political values of his community, calls him back to the 'normal' world. This figure rhymes with that in 'Notes Toward a Supreme Fiction' (CP 397):

A bench was his catalepsy, Theatre
Of Trope. He sat in the park. The water of
The lake was full of artificial things,

Like a page of music, like an upper air,
Like a momentary color, in which swans
Were seraphs, were saints, were changing essences.

The lakeside scene with swans is not an allegory of the revolutionary transformations that Lenin effected, but rather an example of how political thought changes the way we think about space, that is, changes our descriptions of the world immediately before us. That this is indeed the case is witnessed by the fact that both Nietzsche and Lenin are presented here in suspiciously suburban moments, much like those that Stevens himself spent in Elizabeth Park in Hartford and that appeared in the poems. Rainer Maria Rilke thinks about space, albeit with no reference to politics, in a very similar way as one of his poems shows:

Raum greift aus uns und übersetzt die Dinge:
daß dir das Dasein eines Baums gelinge,
wirf Innenraum um ihn, aus jenem Raum,
der in dir west.

[Space reaches *from* us and construes the world:
to know a tree, in its true element,
throw inner space around it, from that pure
abundance in you.]   (Rilke 262–3)

25

Taking this phenomenological tack, we can say that for Stevens the ideas of Nietzsche and Lenin mean nothing unless they mean something first and foremost in this 'Theatre of Trope' (CP 397) – our immediate apprehension of space. The French left-wing philosopher, Henri Lefebvre puts it like this:

> What is an ideology without a space to which it refers, a space which it describes, whose vocabulary and links it makes use of, and whose code it embodies? [. . .] More generally speaking, what we call ideology only achieves consistency by intervening in social space and in its production, and by thus taking on body therein. (44)

It might seem at this stage that I am trying to triangulate Stevens by quotation, but that these two passages from such different writers as Rilke and Lefebvre are pertinent to Stevens helps demonstrate the nature of those tracks between the spaces of political praxis and the artwork that I mentioned earlier. Rilke is all aesthetic exaltation of the natural world – trees, skies, fruit; Lefebvre's end is ultimately the transformation of society. Stevens brings these two spheres into collision. Thinking about the transformations of Marxism means thinking about bouquets, lakes and parks, for if those transformations are not apprehensible in such locales – no matter how distant they seem from theatres of action – then they are chimerical and not worth further consideration. Whereas a critic like Alan Filreis considers that 'Description Without Place' expresses a particular anti-political moment in American society after World War II with its dehistoricisation of the figures of Lenin, Nietzsche and Neruda in this, it is my contention that Stevens, in order to get at the essence of ideologies, reads them against nature (Filreis, *Actual World* 157–8). What Lenin does with the swans characterises accurately what he and his confrères did with those who did not fit into the new political order of Communism.

Stevens's landscapes then are a new version of pastoral by which he tests polities and philosophies against one of the oldest vistas, that of the natural world. To consider new ideas against the city would be fruitless since the city, containing millions and the seat of the latest technologies, is itself a part of the modern. There is no contrast and thus no calibration. Nature, however, provides not a pristine expanse, but a set of terrains that for the most part has remained unchanged by humanity, even while humanity continued to change its interpretation of it. The natural landscape is then 'multi-storied', but plastically constant, thus providing the opportunity to think most clearly about a particular ideology. To examine what Marxism makes of nature, and not how it plans industry or foreign relations, is the most expeditious way of discovering the essence of the ideology.

Here we should remark an important difference between Stevens's representations of nature and those of his Romantic predecessors: that nature is 'storied'
(recall the figure of Triton in the waves) means it is historical. In other words,
rather than being a source of eternal values (moral, aesthetic), nature is the site
of hermeneutic uncertainty, as we are plunged into the awareness that so many
people and so many cultures have made so many different things *of* it. This phrasal
verb 'make of' is useful in that it captures both the idea of aesthetic interpretation
and physical manufacture, both the artworks and industries that look to nature
for raw material. When poets like Wordsworth and Emerson leave the gathered
dwellings of their fellow human beings to range through the landscape in
solitude, they have defined in advance the category into which their perceptions
of nature will fall. The nature they see is delimited negatively, in other words it
is *not* society, *not* the city, *not* modern, *not* industrial. It is 'wilderness', and as
such the site of all the things that Enlightenment society fails to provide: spiritual
feeling, moral values, aesthetic awareness. It is eternal in contrast to the
contingency of the city. It offers a coliseum for pure private emotion, whereas
society imposes the urgency of the newspaper with its mires of political debate
and sensational story. Nature is ahistorical, as unchanging as a Platonic Idea,
refuge and redoubt for the mind troubled by the modern world. It records the
ruins of vanquished empires, thus exhibiting the transience of all human makings
against its unchanging truth. There is a double motion in such a romanticisation
of nature: while in the process of manufacturing a new meaning for nature, these
writers stress its eternal aspect.

These arguments take on special hue when we consider nature and landscape
not just as generic categories but as belonging to the space of America. We must
take into account the history of the US as a colony, and subsequently nation, that
faced the 'wilderness' of the New World, a nature that was very different from
that of Europe. Two landscapes by two American writers will serve to outline
some of the consequences of this distinction. The first is from James Fenimore
Cooper's *The Pioneers* (1823), which takes as its theme the conflicts between the
Native American and European societies about the way land is interpreted.
Cooper, although he registers the resistance offered by the Native Americans to
colonial expansion, is not ultimately their advocate. While he is cognisant of the
faults of white civilisation, in his eyes it is ultimately for the best that it will
triumph. We see this in the opening chapters of his novel. Natty Bumppo is
reluctant to accept that Judge Temple holds a title deed to the huge tracts of land
that surround Templeton, the town named after the judge himself, which allows
him to control it. It means that Bumppo can no longer hunt that ground without
the judge's permission; the fact that this is willingly given is irrelevant to Bumppo.
The previous owners of the land were the Native American tribes and they held
no deeds to it. The very idea of ownership in the judge's sense of the word is alien
to them. This conflict of interpretations of the land provides Cooper with the
springboard for his plot. These descriptions do not provide the consolations of a

27

locus amœnus, rather they are the overture to the conflicts that will entertain us for the remainder of the novel. In the following extract we are travelling with Elizabeth, Judge Temple's daughter, in her carriage as she returns to her town after several years away at school:

> Here and there the hills fell away in long, low points, and broke the sameness of the outline; or setting to the long and wide field of snow, which, without house, tree, fence, or any other fixture, resembled so much spotless cloud settled to the earth. A few dark and moving spots were, however, visible on the even surface, which the eye of Elizabeth knew to be so many sleighs going their several ways, to or from the village. On the western border of the plain, the mountains, though equally high, were less precipitous, and as they receded, opened into irregular valleys and glens, or were formed into terraces and hollows that admitted of cultivation. Although the evergreens still held dominion over many of the hills that rose on this side of the valley, yet the undulating outlines of the distant mountains, covered with forests of beech and maple, gave a relief to the eye, and the promise of a kinder soil. Occasionally, spots of white were discoverable amidst the forests of the opposite hills, which announced, by the smoke that curled over the tops of the trees, the habitations of man, and the commencement of agriculture. These spots were, sometimes, by the aid of united labor, enlarged into what were called settlements; but more frequently were small and insulated; though so rapid were the changes, and so persevering the labors of those who had cast their fortunes on the success of the enterprise, that it was not difficult for the imagination of Elizabeth to conceive they were enlarging under her eye, while she was gazing, in mute wonder, at the alterations that a few short years had made in the aspect of the country. (40)

The landscape that Elizabeth observes from the carriage is not detached from the contingencies of the political and social realities of the time. On the contrary, the fight for 'dominion' between the two civilisations animates it and provides it with a poetic energy. Cooper plays with this idea of dominion as 'wilderness' cedes to 'civilisation'. He is ironic elsewhere in the book about the latter and its careless destruction of the forests and its creatures, but finally is in sympathy with it. However much the book will go on to disparage the wastefulness of the whites, the land here is seen, not through the critical eyes of a Magua, but through those of one of the finest flowers of the conquering race. Elizabeth's is the framing presence: she sets the boundaries of Cooper's sympathy for other races. Without doubt, he feels pity for them as Elizabeth does but he will not look at the landscape through their eyes. The conflicts that swept across the terrain of America in the eighteenth century are the sources of Cooper's fiction, and this contest for the land created his characters, most famously Natty Bumppo. Bumppo is, in so many ways, the frontier itself. He lives between the two cultures. His descriptions of landscape do not occlude its historical aspect as a place contested by different races – they depend on it.

The second landscape I wish to look at is by Cooper's friend and one of the great creators of 'picturesque America', William Cullen Bryant, and is to be found in his poem, 'Thanotopsis':

> When thoughts
> Of the last bitter hour come like a blight
> Over thy spirit, and sad images
> Of the stern agony, and shroud, and pall,
> And breathless darkness, and the narrow house,
> Make thee to shudder, and grow sick at heart; –
> Go forth, under the open sky, and list
> To Nature's teachings, while from all around –
> Earth and her waters, and the depths of air, –
> Comes a still voice [. . .]
>
>   Yet not to thine eternal resting-place
> Shalt thou retire alone, – nor couldst thou wish
> Couch more magnificent. Thou shalt lie down
> With patriarchs of the infant world – with kings,
> The powerful of the earth – the wise, the good,
> Fair forms, and hoary seers of ages past,
> All in one mighty sepulchre. The hills
> Rock-ribbed and ancient as the sun; the vales
> Stretching in pensive quietness between;
> The venerable woods; rivers that move
> In majesty, and the complaining brooks
> That make the meadows green; and, poured round all,
> Old Ocean's grey and melancholy waste –
> Are but the solemn decorations all
> Of the great tomb of man.   (*Poems* 11–12)

Bryant's consolatory campagna, with its 'Italianate sheen' (OP 43), as Stevens called this kind of romanticisation of nature, feels slightly imported. His reference elsewhere in the poem to the Oregon river (now the Columbia) makes it an American landscape, and so it is fair to ask exactly *which* kings and patriarchs are abed in this landscape. Bryant is perhaps gesturing to those of the Old World, thus effortlessly appropriating the American landscape by provisioning it with regal European corpses. This erasure of national difference contributes to the production of the imperial prospect of the poem.

Majesty is easily predicated of the river since the whole poem, with its pro-prietorial gesture (all nature is but a decoration on the tomb of man) excludes

29

the possibility of any contest for this majesty, and it provides a telling contrast with the dominion of the trees in Cooper's landscape. They 'still hold out' against the settlements. In Bryant, there is no place for this kind of tension and conflict. His river merely *looks* majestic. In the way that it excludes the contingencies of the social world, Bryant's landscape is a deathly one. It is a precinct cordoned off by his mellifluous lines and within them we are allowed no glimpse of the historical change that humanity's presence in nature brings about. Moreover Bryant's 'deathly locus' seems very un-American since it conveys no sense of this tract of land partaking of the New World. What I mean by this is that there is no sense of contest in the landscape, no feeling that the imagination must work to appropriate it – instead it is waiting there, to hand, as reliable as a chaise longue upon which to flop down and sigh one's last. Bryant's picturesque gaze is a strategy, a kind of dreamwork that refuses to countenance the darker side of the landscape, and this is borne out by his idealisation of Native American populations during the very century when they were being violently extinguished. In Cooper, the landscape metamorphoses before Elizabeth's eyes and she is surprised by it. The contingencies of the time sweep across her field of vision, and landscape becomes the site where we can see the conflicts of character and civilisation being worked out.

My aim here is not an account of the changing representations of nature from the nineteenth to twentieth centuries in the literature of the United States. However, these two landscapes give a brief indication of the historical context of Stevens's poems of landscape and nature. The novelist and the poet were two of the foremost American romantics of the nineteenth century, which means that they made important contributions to the way that the nature of America was represented in literature and the arts in general. This is especially true of Bryant who edited the eight-volume *Picturesque America* (1872–4). And Cooper's landscape is a healthy complication of this historical context since it precludes the inference that nineteenth-century American representations of nature were monolithic Classical scenes left for a Modernist poet like Stevens to decreate.

Pushed to align the poetry of Wallace Stevens with one of these, most readers would choose Bryant's. They might feel that, like Bryant's, Stevens's work excludes social and historical contingencies in order to maintain a sacred site where the humanist imagination can disport itself untroubled by the messier side of life. Of course, Stevens does not replicate Bryant's occlusion of genocide by idealisation of the landscape and its aborigines – his aestheticisation, they would claim, is different. In a century when the United States was rapidly urbanising, Stevens's poetry of skies and mountains, rivers and seas, could seem escapist, an attempt to avoid a field of experience that is industrial and inarguably modern. Unlike his friend Carl Sandburg, Stevens rarely used the city as location for his poems; the closest he came to this was the park. Such a distaste for urban *materia poetica*, when compared to Sandburg or Hart Crane, appears almost cowardly. But such a characterisation of Stevens is wrong: his recourse to landscape as poetic site bespeaks not cowardice in the face of historical contingency but a knowledge that this contingency could be confronted more fruitfully against the horizon of nature. Stevens's landscapes are indeed special precincts of the imagination, but, as I shall show, they are not static and they are not cordoned off from change as Bryant's is: they metamorphose from the actual to the abstract and back again, and interrogate all human fictions.

It was not until the end of the nineteenth century that the United States was fully mapped, and the sense of uncharted land stretching out from the edges of white civilisation could not but affect the sensibility of some American writers. I would go further and say that this sense that the land has yet to be appropriated by the imagination – that 'imaginative' work must be done to perceive it, to live in its midst as an artist – is one of the constitutional elements of American literature. Although created in one of the longest-colonised parts of America, even the Emersonian sublime, with its metaphysical eye abroad in nature, contains within it the knowledge that the transcendental imagination must work to appropriate and perceive the landscape, colonise it for its own ends. This imagination must make something of the nature that surrounds it, construct a landscape, and the freshness of such literature resides in watching this imagination at work, not in the eternal values it promises that nature will provide. Perhaps it is in this context that we can see Jefferson's Declaration of Independence and Emerson's *Nature* sharing a common source of power. The directness and energy of both texts convey the idea of a limitless expanse of nature to be worked upon by the mattocks and dactyls of Americans. Of course, Emerson's attitudes to the society of his day were complex and did not endorse its direction, but nevertheless in his calls, say, for a national poet it is clear that he sees that an American imagination has yet to appropriate and work the land. And even in *Nature* when he and his 'monocle' go promenading, the route he follows capitalises on the collisions of the eyes' circles with the arrangement of nature. As he turns his head, we feel vast radii sweeping the landscape and arranging it into perspectives, tableaux, moral scenes – and the excitement of this writing is not, like Bryant's, generated by some fixed natural scene that the imagination presents, but by the feeling that these transformations are occurring as one reads nature with Emerson.

Stevens's renovations and rearrangements never present nature as some ahistorical transcendental signified and this is clear from 'Botanist on Alp (No. 1)' (CP 134–5) where he remarks:

Panoramas are not what they used to be.
Claude has been dead a long time
And apostrophes are forbidden on the funicular.
Marx has ruined Nature,
For the moment.

'Notes Toward a Supreme Fiction' is haunted by the idea of a primordial natural space that is obscured by the myriad fictional spaces man has created within it.

Eden could be said to be an earlier version of this. The fictional spaces in which we live and see things through – house, property, state, painting – have created in us an 'ennui' of this first idea. The first idea, the primordial state of nature, the space of the NOT-US is 'Not to be realized because not to / Be seen, not to be loved nor hated because / Not to be realized' (CP 385). It is always historical, as are our attempts to reach back to the first idea.

Here we are at the heart of the natural *abîme*, the muddy centre of Stevens's sublime. Instead of weather, we encounter 'Weather by Franz Hals, // Brushed up by brushy winds in brushy clouds, / Wetted by blue, colder for white' (CP 385). Here as so often in his work, the signifiers of painting, intervening across the poet's contemplation of nature, serve to indicate the difficulty of such a poetic project, and indeed Stevens himself remarked the difficulty he had in writing this canto (L 434). What makes it difficult for us is the tension between the desire to apprehend the first idea, that from which all our ideas and fictions come, and the knowledge that it is unreachable because of the accretions of centuries of mediation (and is indeed a symptom of occupying the moment of the 'late plural'). Negotiating a path between this desire and this knowledge without diminishing the power of either is what this canto (CP 385) accomplishes:

Not to be realized because not to
Be seen, not to be loved nor hated because
Not to be realized. Weather by Franz Hals,

Brushed up by brushy winds in brushy clouds,
Wetted by blue, colder for white. Not to
Be spoken to, without a roof, without

First fruits, without the virginal of birds,
The dark-blown ceinture loosened, not relinquished.
Gay is, gay was, the gay forsythia

And yellow, yellow thins the Northern blue.
Without a name and nothing to be desired,
If only imagined but imagined well.

My house has changed a little in the sun.
The fragrance of the magnolias comes close,
False flick, false form, but falseness close to kin.

It must be visible or invisible,
Invisible or visible or both:
A seeing and unseeing in the eye.

The weather and the giant of the weather,
Say the weather, the mere weather, the mere air:
An abstraction blooded, as a man by thought.

The overall rhetorical gesture is a movement from negation ('Not to be realized')
to affirmation ('the weather, the mere weather'). The negation – the apprehension
of the distance and difficulty of the first idea – is qualified by reference to Hals.
Nature here is caught in the seventeenth century, and this is further emphasised
by 'the virginal of birds'. A virginal is a keyed musical instrument (common in
England in the sixteenth and seventeenth centuries), resembling a spinet, and
'ceinture' is another irredeemably seventeenth-century word. The problem
Stevens faces here is that it is not possible to look at a natural panorama and see
it with an ignorant eye – the process is more complex than the initial no-nonsense
Transcendentalist tone of Canto I would have us believe. The natural object must
first be acknowledged as an historical entity. In the third line of the third tercet,
Stevens brings together the nature of the past, suspended in our seventeenth-
century picturesque notion of it, and that of the present: 'Gay is, gay was, the gay
forsythia'. This change of tense (which is crucial also in 'The Rock') is Stevens's
first step towards a 'cure' of nature, and in the next line – as we step across the
blank interval between tercets – Stevens characteristically reduces the forsythias
to their pure colour against the pure colour of the sky. For Stevens such a reduction
of objects and scenes to their constituent colours and shapes, far from simplifying
issues, signifies a turn of sensibility that marked the modern age. Names are
shucked off in this movement and the desire for some kind of access to the first
idea is gradually satisfied. The responsibility to 'imagine well' is placed on the
human observer facing the natural object.

The tone clearly changes, preparing us for the canto's affirmative end. What
the responsibility consists of is 'A seeing and unseeing in the eye'. Stevens, in
'Examination of the Hero in a Time of War', remarked 'Sight / Is a museum of
things seen' (CP 274). In place of Kant's rose-tinted spectacles and complex per-
ceptual schemata, Stevens necessarily wears over his eyes the huge institution of
a museum, complete with the massive panoply of columns, curators and display
cases. Necessarily, since otherwise he would be avoiding the historicity of nature,
evading the modern difficulty of apprehending it. The conclusion affirms that while
nature can be seen, it is not seen 'as the observer wills'. The observer must apprehend the historicity of nature as part of his perception, and this apprehension must
also become a process of creation and decreation, 'A seeing and unseeing in the eye'.

This dialogue between the poem and Hals's signifiers registers the historicity
of nature and also the distance the poet must traverse to apprehend its absence
and its lessons: he must immerse himself in dialogue between verbal and pictorial
representations to redeem the imagination – and what is this redemption but an
empowerment exceeding the limits and divisions of existing knowledge and praxis?
But this empowerment is different again from Emerson's: the Transcendentalist

would reduce the natural world to idea. Stevens, on the other hand, privileges the power of nature to change the human observer. Stevens is wary of reducing any part of the natural world to his own conscious mode of being, of offering a final representation of the natural object.

And even though Stevens acknowledges the historicity of landscape in a way that Emerson doesn't, and even though he refuses to abandon the concerns of the community when he wanders out beneath the open skies, he still wishes to leave room for the kind of exaltation that Emerson experienced when walking across the heath at the beginning of *Nature*.[1] It is, to use a favourite collocation of Stevens, a good. A nature poetry of his kind affords the poet a space to inhale the healths of the open air and the wide prospect of nature, while realising that these moments are cathected by a public context. This is no crude politicisation of nature – landscape is still a place of 'diviner health' and ecstatic emotion – but it does suggest a set of complex negotiations that the poet must undertake, not in order to sing Nature over humankind, rather to say that on the deepest level we are always thinking politically and ethically even when we are in its midst. A short poem from *Ideas of Order* (CP 125–6) has two figures climbing up a mountain to find heroic images. Their expectations of romantic revelation are disappointed:

> Instead there was this tufted rock
> Massively rising high and bare [. . .]
>
> . . . .
>
> There was the cold wind and the sound
> It made, away from the muck of the land
> That they had left, heroic sound
> Joyous and jubilant and sure.

The title of the poem, which Stevens once said 'so definitely represents my way of thinking' (L 293), is of course 'How to Live. What to Do'.

Chapter 2

Stevens and nature poetry

1

The problem with many recent readings of Stevens is that they are suspicious of statements like that in his letter to Hi Simons: 'The "ever jubilant weather" is not a symbol. We are physical beings in a physical world; the weather is one of things that we enjoy, one of the unphilosophical realities' (L 348–9). Talk of jubilation and the weather and, elsewhere in Stevens, exaltation, seems suspiciously ahistorical. Could there be hankerings after the bogey of 'universalism' lurking in such expressions? In the case of many poets in the Romantic tradition the hankerings are definitely there, but such is not the case with Stevens. The pastoral space in which these jubilations and exaltations are experienced is also the space in which Stevens looks at politics and human history; further, it is the space that often occasions such thinking. Poetry must engage 'the great interests of man: air and light, the joy of having a body, the voluptuousness of looking' (Stevens quoting the Italian philosopher, Mario Rossi [CP 136]), but at the same time it must talk of Lenin, revolution, social change and organisation, which are also interests of man, albeit affording less pleasure. It is within the great amphitheatre of air and light that Stevens considers Lenin and the rest and we do his poetry a great disservice by not recognising the oblique ways in which his political pastoral works. It is not ideological, by which I mean that it does not have implicit within it a particular set of values. Rather it provides a horizon against which all ideologies and their mechanisms can be considered. Again, this presupposition of a space outside ideology smacks somewhat of universalism. But Stevens is more subtle than to try to import a value-system while pretending to be beyond such matters. He is not beyond them but needs a space to think about them, as do we all. Steven Miskinis says that 'for Stevens the imagination is never outside or distant from the political – rather, it is distinctive from the political – it opens the very possibility of such a distinction' (225). My terms are different but the drift is the same: the natural spaces in Stevens's poetry are where the energies of the political are directed in order for both poet and reader to see them more clearly. Our own choice of medium for such theorising (and seeing is, incidentally, etymology of the word 'theory') is critical prose. But as Fredric Jameson's essay shows, it is through landscapes that Stevens provides us with the room to theorise.

But before I go any further I wish to explain my use of the terms landscape, land and nature. Emerson said in *Nature* that nature was everything that was 'NOT ME' but went on in the same essay to discuss it as something that is made up of rivers, mountains, fields, horizons, clouds, and emphatically not cities and the society of other people.[1] Similarly, as Voros points out, when Stevens says 'reality', more often than not he means a landscape, some scene from nature (11). (Often what is sufficient is something taken from nature, for instance flowers or fruit.) Even 'An Ordinary Evening in New Haven', which is ostensibly set in a city, significantly turns, as I shall show, to nature and landscape at the poem's end. Frank Lentricchia comments that unlike Emerson, 'Stevens's terms are antitranscendental and naturalistic, atheistic and aestheticist; but with Emerson he tends to believe that these moments of vitality cannot happen in the streets of our cities' (*Modernist Quartet* 137).

We associate landscape most readily with landscape painting, depictions of natural scenes arranged by an artist. In contrast to this, nature seems less 'constructed', and yet there is no end-run to an unmediated view of it – it too is a cultural construct. This may seem to contradict my earlier remarks on the appropriation of uncharted wilderness by the imagination in America. But these uncharted tracts have already been designated as 'wilderness', and the idea of 'wilderness' is also a cultural construct, a way of seeing land that is possible only if you know what it is defined by – civilisation. The confrontation between the American imagination and nature is not primordial though it has all the appearance of being so. The American wilderness was seen *for what it was not* – because it was emphatically not the cities and countrysides of Europe, therefore it was deemed 'wilderness'. Stevens meditates on such differences in 'Anecdote of the Jar' where the jar seems to create the wilderness itself. We are tempted to think that the wilderness was merely wilderness before the jar was placed on the hill, but 'wilderness' can only be defined negatively in contrast with that which is not wild, that is, the plain, civilised jar.

Figures in Stevens's poems are often hubristic enough to think that they can broker a primordial deal between themselves and nature, a deal that bypasses the aggregate of cultural constructs that make up our ideas of it. Crispin, in his search for an autochthonous poetry that correctly balances one's soil and one's intelligence, is one such. After following his adventures across the Atlantic and through the Americas, Stevens clips his relation shut quite brusquely, revealing an impatience with Crispin's ambitions that not even irony can satisfy. But yet Stevens returns to such figures throughout the rest of *Harmonium*, and though they never realise their ambitions, he sees the thwarting of them as instructive. They play a decisive role in a poetic development that concerns itself with the processes of the appropriation of nature for various goals. Because nature for Stevens is the site of the contest of imaginative fictions, his landscapes are dynamic like Cooper's – nature is not a coulisse to be rolled on for the performance of the poem, it is a zone that the poems contest. Characters like Crispin, whose imaginations work to appropriate nature, introduce an agency and propose landscape as the place where different fictions contend with each other.

However, unlike in Cooper, Stevens's poems do not take a particular historical moment when land is being contested. There are more ways than this to apprehend landscape in its historical aspect and avoid the deathly campagna of Bryant. In Stevens, philosophers, statesmen, revolutionaries, swains, ascetics, captains and colonisers step forward to try to make something of the land in which they find themselves. They work this land with their constructions, and they must engage other constructions even if it is only to clear them away. (Crispin has come to 'A still new continent in which to dwell' and the work his imagination must do is 'to drive away / The shadow of his fellows from the skies, / And, from their stale intelligence released, / To make a new intelligence prevail' [CP 37].) As Stevens recounts their successes and failures, that land is revealed as polyvalent, most truly revealed in the phases of difference between these contending fictions. Bryant's eternal coulisse becomes just one more episode, yet another fiction to be dismantled and ironised. Thus Stevens registers the historical aspect of nature, but, more importantly for my argument, he also shows how the move from Classical scenes to their ironisation is part of the changing ways that communities think about themselves, change and exchange the images and figures that best describe what and who they are. Like his first botanist on the Alps, he knows that a change in a political system entails a change in how the mountains appear to us.

In this chapter, I shall outline two critical accounts of the place of landscape in Stevens's poetry and then go on to compare his work with that of Robinson Jeffers, widely known as one of the foremost nature poets of the twentieth century. Concluding with readings of 'Dry Loaf' and 'Like Decorations in a Nigger Cemetery', I shall show Stevens the nature poet at work as he encompasses moments of exaltation and despair, as well as wider considerations of human society.

2

Fredric Jameson and Bonnie Costello have discussed the part that landscape plays in Stevens's poetry. Costello, arguing against readings such as Harold Bloom's and Joseph Carroll's that figure the poet as a triumphalist of the human imagination over the contingencies of the material world, has shown how landscape represents a base to which Stevens often returns when consoling fictions fall away ('Adequacy' 204, 216–17). She shows also how Stevens reacted against the 'totalizing space of classical and romantic landscape' by revealing its 'constructedness and hence the contingency of [its] vision' ('Adequacy' 211). 'Stevens' landscapes are', she argues, 'pragmatic and provisional, affording aesthetic and emotional if not intellectual arrival', a background that 'defines not only an opportunity for the imagination but the limits of its independence as well' (204). Such a fresh emphasis in a reading of the poems, as Costello points out, implies a relocation of Stevens within certain cultural and social contexts, since attitudes towards landscape played such an important role in the construction of the national identity of the United States. Stevens's provisional paysages begin to represent a way of reassessing the uses to which ideas of landscape are put, whether they be to bolster a national mythology or generate a tourist industry. Our landscapes are also the primary means through which our attitudes towards nature as a whole are formed. These attitudes perhaps owe more to this totalising space of Classicism and Romanticism, which Stevens, in Costello's reading, tries to disrupt, insofar as we still presume to dominate nature for our own ends, whether to build nations, to provide holiday breaks in 'unspoilt' natural surroundings or to extract raw materials for the purposes of industry. In each of these instances the message is clear that nature is at our disposal.

Jameson's essay would seem to promise to lead us in a similar direction with its opening gambit: 'Stevens' *only* content, from the earliest masterpieces of *Harmonium* all the way to the posthumous [*sic*] Rock, is landscape' (178). But by the end of the same paragraph we see that there is a deep divergence between him and Costello:

> In Stevens, nature is, however, nothing but a given, a ready-made occasion for speech – birds, wind, mountains, the sun, always ready to hand whenever poetic speech needs some kind of objective content for its own production. (179)

Stevens's landscapes are 'laundered of their cultural and social semantics' (179), and his poetry, which uses these landscapes merely 'as a set of neutral counters for the exercise of poetic speech', designates nothing beyond itself. (In the context of his critical approach, the pun on 'laundering' is admirable as it passes off the poetry as some kind of 'funny money'.) This autoreferentiality does not, he goes on to say, collapse into the usual stances of high modernism, but is the moment when 'an unusual permutation takes place [. . .] in which "the theory of poetry" becomes at one with "the life of poetry" (190). Stevens's poetry, discoursing on nothing beyond itself becomes the moment that poetry 'in its traditional sense, dies and is transformed into something historically new', Theory (191). By taking nature as his subject, Jameson argues, Stevens is able to avoid the very issues that Costello claims Stevens's poetry engages (Costello, 'Adequacy' 207). Stevens, on Jameson's reading, replicates the gestures and visions of Classicism that viewed nature as a resource for human needs, be they æsthetic or social. Clearly, he would align his work with a meditative lyric like 'Thanotopsis'. If Stevens wants to write poetry then nature is standing waiting to be used (one thinks of Bryant's 'couch') as a pliant subject that will not disrupt his discourse on the true theme, that of poetry itself.

Jameson's essay though published in 1984 has made little impression on Stevens criticism. The most likely reason for this is the inaccuracy of the central statement that the poetry discourses on nothing beyond itself: after reading the books of James Longenbach and Alan Filreis this seems anything but perspicacious. Nevertheless, there is the wonderful intuitive observation (which unfortunately leads him to contradict himself) that Stevens's landscapes are locales of ur-Theory. The contradiction resides in the fact that Jameson on the one hand says that Stevens's poems are about nothing beyond themselves, yet are the beginning of Theory. But what is Theory but the consideration of the relations between history, politics and culture? It is true that a lot of the theory of the 1980s seemed to be discoursing on nothing beyond itself, but the best theorists always knew that something more was at stake. For instance, in *Canons and Consequences*, Charles Altieri bluntly states: 'In my text I project a hope that the effort to get theory right is also in a limited domain an effort to get a life right, in the sense of taking responsibility for the values that govern one's work' (vii). The 'something more' is a concern with ethics and culture, and their interconnections, at the deepest levels, i.e., how should society organise itself? For what reasons should its members be told to sacrifice their lives (war? capital punishment?)? And how, in the light of these issues, should communities represent themselves to themselves through the work of culture? These questions are fundamental for Stevens, and he engages them in the space of nature.

Jameson goes on to say that Stevens lacks 'the visionary sense of many of the great nature poets, for whom the momentary epiphanies of place and object world are rare events, to be preserved over against the encroaching destruction of Nature as well as the alienating features of city or man-made environment' (178–9). But although Jameson's comparison of Stevens with visionary nature poets seems like a reproach, he is at pains to say that his comments should not 'be taken as criticisms, nor even yet as an ideological critique, of Stevens' work' (179). He would agree that Stevens doesn't employ landscape in the way that, say, Turner did (the British painter disrupted the charmed space of picturesque *vedute* to expose the social tensions of the time, much to the displeasure of contemporaneous critics, for example see Helsinger). But his comparison of Stevens with the great visionary nature poets who use nature to castigate civilisation (in other words, who use nature as an instrument of ideology) leads him to state that Stevens's poetry designates nothing beyond itself (191). The idea of nature qua ideological instrument is indeed anathema to Stevens, but it hardly implies that Stevens uses landscape and the seasons merely as pretexts for a poetic utterance that has no true subject but itself.

What I wish to do in this chapter is investigate the polarity that Jameson sets up here in order to come to a better idea of what kind of nature poetry Stevens writes, and the particular way that it includes within it questions of ideology, politics and history. Arguing this point is not just a matter of setting one critic of Stevens over another, but should extend our awareness of Stevens as a poet who is continually concerned with the orientation of the individual and the community within the landscapes and metamorphoses of the natural world. W. J. T. Mitchell has argued that that landscape 'naturalizes a cultural and social construction, representing an artificial world as if it were simply given and inevitable, and it also makes that representation operational by interpellating its beholder in some more or less determinate relation to its givenness as sight and site' (Introduction 2). Thus Stevens's representations of landscape, which do not accord to our received notions of nature poetry, can be seen as challenging such a 'naturalisation' of nature.

Robinson Jeffers is a poet whom I consider to fit Jameson's description of a 'great nature poet'. As Jeffers himself states, 'to feel / Greatly, and understand greatly, and express greatly, the natural / Beauty, is the sole business of poetry' (*Selected Poems* 94). F. O. Matthiessen, who happened to be reviewing one of Jeffers's books with *Ideas of Order* in 1936, remarked: 'When Mr. Stevens comments on the present state of the world, you are not given Mr Jeffers's melodramatic vision of all mankind plunging down the hill to a darkened sea' (606). Jeffers felt that it was his mission to hymn the superiority of the natural world over the world that humanity was creating for itself in the forms of cities and towns and that could only end in apocalypse. The poetry is continually embattled: 'civilization is a transient sickness' that in its lifetime goes about destroying the beauties of the natural world (*Selected Poetry of Robinson Jeffers* 363). In one of his most anthologised poems, 'Carmel Point', he recoils in disgust at the construction of suburban houses in a place of great natural beauty, and is haunted by memories of what that place was once like before being subordinated to social needs. These buildings clearly represent for him 'the alienating features of city [and] man-made environment' that are encroaching on nature and making its beauty hard to apprehend (Jameson 179). The poem ends with the instruction that, for all this, we must seek out nature in the place where it quietly endures these forays upon it, and try to imitate its attitude. Nature is a wise presence that is represented as waiting for the disappearance of humanity: 'It knows the people are a tide / That swells and in time will ebb, and all / Their works dissolve' and until that time nature's beauty hides itself. With relish, Jeffers himself looks forward to the destruction of humanity itself since this is the moment when nature will reassert itself. The following passage from 'Their Beauty Has More Meaning' illustrates this point:

> And when the whole human race
> Has been like me rubbed out, they will still be here: storms, moon and ocean,
> Dawn and the birds. And I say this: their beauty has more meaning
> Than the whole human race and the race of birds.

> (*Selected Poems* 77)

Reading his poetry of praise for nature we are continually told that the destructive powers of humanity are in the offing and could make incursions at any moment. The moments that Jeffers cherishes are those when nature is able to manifest itself as something pristine, something that humanity has not yet tarnished or appropriated. And even in a poem like 'The Place for No Story' when such a moment occurs, it is not sufficient for Jeffers that such a moment is witnessed, but the *volta* of the poem, the hinge round which it swings, is the statement that humanity has not yet made its mark on the spot (*Selected Poems* 55). In this poem the 'human presence' is only mildly destructive: it would 'dilute the lonely self-watchful passion'. But what this poem shares with others is his sense that human agency is always lying in ambush to destroy the beauties of nature. In poem after poem (apart from the long narratives) the turning point occurs about such contrasts: nature is beautiful and will endure, humanity is sordid and, although it temporarily threatens nature, it will eventually be extinguished. No doubt it will, but to be continually told so in poetry or out of it is tedious.

And not only does Jeffers adequately fit Jameson's description but in so many ways he would seem to represent the exact opposite of a poet like Stevens. For Jeffers, the building of his house and tower on the coast of California was a poetic act in itself. He saw the United States as the endpoint of Western civilisation: it had originated in the Orient and would end in the West (*Selected Poems* 40). Thus his tower gave him a vantage point not only on the Pacific Ocean but also on a vision of the world after humanity had vacated it. Stevens's house on Westerly Terrace in Hartford, which he certainly did not build himself, stands in stark contrast to this. It represents the bourgeois ideal of the successful business-man who does not think that 'civilization is a transient sickness', but on the contrary feels quite good about the whole human project. Echoing this is Jeffers's deep-seated misanthropy as against Stevens's appreciation of the work of the human imagination in its many different manifestations.[2] While Jeffers consoles himself with visions of the erasure of humanity from the earth, Stevens sings the praises of the major man. Another difference, which would have been very noticeable during the years that both poets were at the height of their powers, was their differing public profiles. Jeffers was a hugely popular poet. *Tamar and Other Poems* (1924) was published to wide critical acclaim and a full-length bibliography of his work came out only eight years after his first successful collection (Carpenter 43). The book, enlarged to *Roan Stallion, Tamar, and Other Poems* (1925), was reprinted many times in the following years (Carpenter 40). In contrast with this, the first year's royalties for *Harmonium* brought in Stevens the princely sum of $6.70 (L 243) and – for the most part – indifferent reviews. And while Stevens published very little over the next few years, by 1929 Jeffers had published four volumes in four successive years.

Stevens and Jeffers also differ in their attitudes to poetry itself. Jeffers, in the introduction to a selection of his poems in the late 1950s, reflects on his own poetry and its place in poetry in general:

Long ago, before anything included here was written, it became evident to me that poetry – if it was to survive at all – must reclaim some of the power and reality that it was so hastily surrendering to prose. The modern French poetry of that time, and the most 'modern' of the English poetry, seemed to me thoroughly defeatist, as if poetry were in terror of prose, and desperately trying to save its soul from the victor by giving up its body. It was becoming slight and fantastic, abstract, unreal, eccentric; and was not even saving its soul, for these are generally anti-poetic qualities. It must reclaim substance and sense, and physical and psychological reality. This feeling has been basic in my mind since then. (*The Selected Poetry of Robinson Jeffers* xiv)

The diatribe is clearly directed against Eliot, but it is easy to imagine that Jeffers would not object to a book like *Harmonium* being described as 'fantastic, abstract, unreal, eccentric'. The poems of Stevens's first book, with their filigree ironies, contrast starkly with a poem like 'Tamar', which is the narrative of the incestuous and murderous Cauldwell family and is set in contemporary California. That poem is closer to the fiction of Steinbeck and the drama of O'Neill than the lucubrations of the East Coast insurance executive. Jeffers clearly wants poetry to be *about* something and for poets to cease 'from being the astute calligraphers of congealed daydreams, the hunters of cerebral phosphorescences', to quote the epigraph from 'Reply to Papini' (CP 446). When we read Jeffers's work we are supposed to feel his muscular grasp of his subject and be impressed by the strong lone voice speaking the truth while other writers simply cannot rise to this mark: he strives for the heroic tone. And although little critical attention is given to him now, there is an energy in his poetry of a kind that will never be found in Stevens. For all his hatred of mankind, he has moments that are valuable for their brutal honesty and power of direct expression. 'Hurt Hawks' stands as an example of these qualities; it is a poem where Jeffers's objectionable misanthropy is convincingly integrated in a poem of great pathos and beauty. Unfortunately, such moments are not abundant and quite often we find the same thoughts recycled in poem after poem. The typical curve that a Jeffers lyric takes is from meditation on the natural world to a comparison of this with humanity in which the latter always comes off badly. After reading twenty such poems it is difficult to find reasons to read on.

Stevens displays no such tortured messianism. If we compare some of his playful thoughts on poetry in the Adagia with Jeffers's pronouncements in his foreword, the difference in hardly needs expatiation:

The poet makes silk dresses out of worms. (OP 184)

Merit in poets is as boring as merit in people. (OP 184)

Words are the only melodeon. (OP 196)

Poetry is a pheasant disappearing in the brush. (OP 198)

42

And if we go on to compare a poem like 'The Place For No Story' with lines like the following, it would seem as though their differences are incontestable (CP 75):

> Damned universal cock, as if the sun
> Was blackamoor to bear your blazing tail.

Stevens is playful, Jeffers is in earnest. Stevens is a self-conscious artist, Jeffers aspires to the primitive. Stevens dons masks, Jeffers draws no line between his speakers and his personal voice. Stevens ignores social concerns, Jeffers wants to be America's Cassandra. Stevens has been accommodated within the complex critical debates on Modernism, Jeffers hasn't. Stevens likes humanity, Jeffers hates it. Stevens had no subject, Jeffers had.

The battlelines are drawn. Further confirmation can be gained by a comparison of two poems by these authors that have a similar setting and speakers but widely differing conclusions: Stevens's 'Chocorua to Its Neighbour' and Jeffers's 'The Inquisitors'. Jeffers's poem tells the story of a horseman, Azevedo, riding into a valley and coming upon the strange sight of two mountains inquiring into the nature of humanity by dismembering certain citizens of the valley. The horseman plays only a minor part – he is like the small figures in the corners of *vedute* that point to the panorama depicted. He is our eyes and ears: through him we witness what the mountains do and say.

> He heard the rumble of a voice, heavy not loud, saying, 'I gathered some,
> You can inspect them.' One of the hills moved a huge hand
> And poured its contents on a table-topped rock that stood in the firelight;
>   men and women fell out;
> Some crawled and some lay quiet; the hills leaned to eye them. One said: 'It
>   hardly seems possible
> Such fragile creatures could be so noxious.' Another answered,
> 'True, but we've seen. But it is only recently they have the power.' The third
>   answered, 'That bomb?'
> 'Oh,' he said, ' – and the rest.' He reached across and picked up one of those
>   mites from the rock, and held it
> Close to his eyes, and very carefully with finger and thumbnail peeled it: by
>   chance a young female
> With long black hair: it was too helpless even to scream.

(Selected Poems 81–2)

They calmly go on to split 'its' skull to see if the seed of humanity is contained there, and all they find is a 'drop of marrow'. Inquiring further they peel, crack, toast, and 'split their bodies from the crotch upward / To stare inside', but without any further illumination. They yawn (such a blasé gesture contrasting nicely with their bloody investigations) and lope off southward, having concluded that

43

humanity will probably destroy itself and life will begin again. This is fine by them. Jeffers so luxuriates in the description of these blithe dismemberments that it is hard to feel that its motivation is didactic rather than a desire to indulge his own vivacious misanthropy.

Stevens's 'Chocorua to Its Neighbour' (CP 296–302) is very different. The poem begins with a grand flourish in which the mountain Chocorua meditates on the very fact of its own speech (bringing it closer to Jameson's characterisation):

> To speak quietly at such a distance, to speak
> And to be heard is to be large in space,
> That, like your own, is large, hence, to be part
> Of sky, of sea, large earth, large air.

The mountain will continue in this vein in Section XIX, letting Stevens gently ironise his own ventriloquy in the poem. Jeffers's fable, insistent on conveying its message in the most gruesome terms possible, has no time for such self-conscious artistry. The figure that collects itself together on the top of the mountain is, in Stevens's poem, a major man, a type for civilisation's leaders – 'The captain squalid on his pillow, the great / Cardinal, saying the prayers of earliest day [. . .] the scholar, / Whose green mind bulges with complicated hues: // True trans-figurers fetched out of the human mountain' (CP 300). (Whereas Alan Filreis sees this catalogue of figures as democratic in the spirit of Whitman, I rather see it as apologia for an elite: all the figures are leaders of one sort or another [*Actual World* 60].) The hilltop figure himself seems like a figure fetched out of the physical elements ('He was a shell of dark blue glass, or ice, / Or air collected in a deep essay, / Or light embodied [. . .]' [CP 297]). In the sense that the figure is formed from natural elements in the image of man, it represents a kind of interface between the large natural presence of Chocorua and civilisation. As early as Section II Stevens sets a civilisational context for this poem about mountains with such lines as 'The armies are forms in number, as cities are. / The armies are cities in movement' (CP 296). He brings the poem back to these terms in Section XXIV as the poem is reaching its conclusion that confirms this figure's worth in majestic phrases and ends with Chocorua's admiration for this 'Political tramp with an heraldic air':

> How singular he was as man, how large,
> If nothing more than that, for the moment, large
> In my presence, the companion of presences
> Greater than mine, of his demanding, head
> And, of human realizings, rugged roy . . .

Whereas in 'The Inquisitors' the mountains go tramping off disgusted with humankind, in 'Chocorua' nature and civilisation, a mountain landscape and a major man, reach a momentary accord. Stevens dons a mountain-mask to make his point. Even when making serious points his ventriloquies are playful and self-ironising. Refracted through these different ventriloquies (Stevens pretending to be a mountain, and nested inside this monologue, the mountain delivering the major man's monologue) is an affirmation of the relations between humanity and nature, however evanescent and, to use Costello's term, provisional. Stevens lets the mountain endorse the 'true transfigurers' of civilisation, such as the captain and the cardinal. It is a masterful apologia for a cultural elitism that believes that if these eminent figures are influenced by the major man then civilisation is steered well.

Hawks and eagles were images of nobility for Jeffers. Their viewpoint represented the eye of nature itself, uncluttered by human emotions like mercy and love. (In 'Hurt Hawks' he says he would sooner, 'except the penalties, kill a man than a hawk'.) Stevens, in 'Some Friends from Pascagoula' (CP 126–7), ironises this practice that takes a creature from nature and gives it symbolic force. ('Lions in Sweden' [CP 124] also shows the way that natural forms are taken out of nature and given meanings by man.) The poem's speaker is instructing the subaltern figures of 'Cotton' and 'black Sly' to talk about the eagle as 'a sovereign sight'.

> Describe with deepened voice
> And noble imagery
> His slowly-falling round
> Down to the fishy sea.

What Stevens indicates is that the 'nobility' is not a feature of the bird but is caused by the pathetic fallacies of the imagery and the tone of voice used by Cotton and Sly. It is a human quality that is imposed on nature. Curiously the two 'pathetic falsifiers' are *commanded* in this poem, as though Stevens were instructing them in an obsolete typology. This would imply some cynicism on his part, and yet it is difficult to hear cynicism. The speaker is clearly in thrall to his own constructions also, as though he wishes the subalterns to confirm his delusion. This then undercuts the power relation implied by the imperatives, as the speaker appears imaginatively weak: he cannot face the blank of the natural world without ethical significance.

Unlike Jeffers, he refuses to use nature as a resource for furnishing the human imagination with a set of stock symbols. For the latter, nature has one meaning: it is the material base that will survive when 'the transient sickness' of civilisation has passed. Its natural beauty seems only to be a function of this attitude: that is, nature is beautiful only because it is not humanity. Considered as such, its role in Jeffers's poetry is unchanging. It is always to hand to chide the hubris of humanity and this fixed attitude towards nature is the cause of the repetitions of his poetry. In contrast, Stevens's nature is a site where interpretations incessantly emerge and exchange themselves for others. Occasionally the imaginative appropriation of nature has a tragic aspect (as in 'The Plain Sense of Things', or in the movement between 'Dutch Graves in Bucks County' and 'No Possum, No Sop, No Taters'), sometimes comical ('Apostrophe to Vincentine' or 'The Comedian as the Letter C') and often it is figured as an accord with a particular individual who matches the landscape or mood of nature at a particular time ('Anecdote of Men by the Thousand'). No doubt this kind of fluidity is what prompted Jameson's contrast of Stevens's outlook with 'the visionary sense of many of the great nature poets'. In Stevens there is no unchanging line of demarcation between humanity and nature. Sometimes looking at a landscape, the tune hummed by the viewer can be the rhythm of the changing scene (CP 243). Sometimes the viewer is violently pulled apart, his eyesight falling to earth (CP 294). Perhaps Jameson would say that this inconsistency, this very unwillingness to fix its value, reveals that Stevens cares for it in a different way from a poet like Jeffers, who values it above the incursions of civilisation.

But Stevens (to turn Berryman on his head) was wider. He *includes* the concerns of a Jeffers in the scope of his poetry. Take a poem like 'Landscape with Boat' (CP 241–3) where Stevens criticises a figure like Jeffers who aspires to an unmediated relationship with landscape. The 'anti-master-man, floribund ascetic' is someone who doesn't realise that his own observation of the landscape is also an agency in it and that the truth of landscape cannot be broached until the figure admits this. As is obvious in 'The Place for No Story' Jeffers does not consider his own presence at Sovranes Creek a human presence. He talks of the site as though it were pristine, discounting the way that his poem has represented it. Jeffers's world-weariness gives him access, he thinks, to the finished gaze of nature, which can no longer be cajoled into believing human fictions. He now stands, in Stevens's phrase, 'At the neutral centre, the ominous element, / The single colored, colorless primitive' (CP 242), his gaze 'fool-proof and permanent'. He has brushed away 'the colossal illusion of heaven' (CP 241) with its projection of human morality on the sky. But Stevens's poem, although it discusses such a figure, cannot indulge its aspirations for long:

> It was not as if the truth lay where he thought,
> Like a phantom, in an uncreated night.
> It was easier to think it lay there. If
> It was nowhere else, it was there and because
> It was nowhere else, its place had to be supposed,
> Itself had to be supposed, a thing supposed
> In a place supposed, a thing that he reached
> In a place that he reached, by *rejecting* what he saw
> And *denying* what he heard.   (Italics mine)

Seen through the lens of Stevens's poem Jeffers's monumental truth becomes 'a thing supposed / In a place supposed'. Jeffers's landscape is monovalent; it closes possibilities and is based on the 'rejection' and 'denial' of things seen and heard. There is no more work for the imagination to do in a landscape by Jeffers. The latter is blind to the many selves and sensuous worlds that are available to those who do not try to extract a moral for their times from the landscape. Whereas Stevens follows the way in which the imagination expends energy metamorphosing the landscape, tracing the vicissitudes of its project for dominion, Jeffers's landscapes are *faits accomplis*. For Stevens, as a poet who is open to these possibilities, figures who close them off exert a fascination.

But despite the differing breadths of vision, both poets often hold that nature is the centre of things and human fictions are ec-centric. For Stevens this is demonstrated by the way that nature can accommodate so many fictions, which sometimes are conflicting. For Jeffers, nature's centrality is apprehended by the fact that it is inhuman. His advice in 'Carmel Point' is that we must stop thinking that man is the centre of things:

> We must uncenter our minds from ourselves;
> We must unhumanize our views a little, and become confident
> As the rock and ocean that we were made from.　　　　(*Selected Poems* 102)

This is prompted by his disgust at the suburban houses that are being built on the point. Stevens's feeling of the centrality of nature is not so misanthropic, and yet on some occasions he has nothing but scorn for the way that humanity appropriates nature to bolster fictions of its own capability and strength. (At other moments when it appears that the observer is genuinely open to nature's possibilities, Stevens expresses approbation, as in 'Contrary Theses (II)', 'Infanta Marina', or 'Tea at the Palaz of Hoon'.)

The people in 'On the Adequacy of Landscape' (CP 243) want to avoid the discursive wings of the owl at night because those wings assert certain 'central things', reminding the people of their ec-centricity and the fact that they 'shrink to an insensible, / Small oblivion' in the midst of the landscape. The *adequate* landscape of the title is another landscape that is sung by another bird, the cock in the morning, who wakes them. (Costello, although she takes title of her essay from this poem, does not discuss it.) The way this bird's song mediates the landscape confirms their delusion that the strength of the sun supports them and that this limited landscape (sung by the morning bird) is 'the extent of what they are'. (Singing landscapes into being will not seem strange to readers of 'The Idea of Order at Key West'.) Stevens concludes the poem with an ironic reminder that these are the same people who were frightened by the owl that evoked a landscape which shrank them to 'an insensible, / Small oblivion'. Stevens mocks the attitude of the people who consider themselves central: the night landscape of the owl is the true centre.

'The essential poem at the centre of things' is what renovates the perception of landscape in 'A Primitive Like an Orb' (CP 440–3). In Stevens the central or essential poem is not an actual poem but would be better described as the Platonic Idea of the poem in which written poems partake. It is also an interface for humanity and nature. The demarcations between the 'central things' of the landscape and the 'central poem' become blurred. The lover, the believer and the poet are 'ec-centric' to this centrality and yet each one is 'part, but part, tenacious particle'. These figures 'celebrate the central poem' to the point where

> the used-to earth and sky, and the tree
> And cloud, the used-to tree and used-to cloud,
> Lose the old uses that they made of them,
> And they: these men, and earth and sky, inform
> Each other by sharp informations, sharp,
> Free knowledges, secreted until then,
> Breaches of that which held them fast. It is
> As if the central poem became the world,

> VI
> And the world the central poem, each one the mate
> Of the other [. . .]

At this point it is worth recalling the two nineteenth-century landscapes I discussed in the first chapter. In this passage we see him describing the way one idea supersedes another and precipitates a new way of seeing earth and sky and tree, and also how such seeing has great import for how communities think about themselves. In 'On the Adequacy of Landscape' Stevens presents us with an image of a community somehow abutting on these changes between the nightscape and day-scape. It is clear that the negotiation of the centrality and eccentricity of the two landscapes has significant implications for this group of people. They are 'held fast' and need a poet, a lover or believer to help them breach their enclosures. These people are similar to those of 'Wild Ducks, People and Distances' who say: 'We grew used so soon, too soon, to earth itself, / As an element; to the sky, as an element. / People might share but were never an element, // Like earth and sky' (CP 328–29). In 'A Primitive' the central poem is something outside that which holds them fast, in the landscape, inhering in the earth, sky, trees and clouds.

In 'The Well Dressed Man with a Beard' (CP 247) Stevens refers to the relationship of a certain kind of poetic speech with a constructed landscape. Elements have been 'rejected' and 'denied' and brushed beyond the edge of our vision.

> If the *rejected* things, the things *denied*,
> Slid over the western cataract [. . .]

a speech
Of the self that must sustain itself on speech,
One thing remaining, infallible, would be
Enough. Ah! douce campagna of that thing!   (Italics mine)

'Rejecting' and 'denying' elements of the landscape were the activities of the 'anti-master-man' of 'Landscape with Boat' four pages before this in the *Collected Poems*. That person had to exclude parts of the landscape to reach his truth, and this was viewed negatively by Stevens. In 'Well Dressed Man' Stevens acknowledges that the poetic speech that Jameson ascribes to him would be possible if certain perceptions of landscape were to disappear into the cataract and be secreted from vision. Then the poet would indeed have a 'douce campagna' instead of a landscape teeming with interpretive possibilities, exceeding the squamous mind. Stevens is suitably ironic about this prospect. Perhaps the well-dressed man with a beard is one of the Fireside poets of the nineteenth century who rejected and denied the more distasteful elements of nature to present a 'douce campagna'. Perhaps it is Bryant himself, who sports a beard on the frontispiece of my edition of his poems. The landscapes of Stevens's poetry are neither such campagnas nor the monovalent ones of Jeffers, which are the instruments of his misanthropy. The title also indicates the way that Stevens is aware that landscapes are often employed by certain social formations: here the man of the title is respectably bourgeois and as a result his landscape is too. It is a *genteel* landscape that is predicated upon 'rejecting' and 'denying' the more anarchic elements of nature. This calls to mind Henri Lefebvre's comment quoted in Chapter One that every ideology has its own space, that is, gives different values to various object relations. Such arrangement of the space of landscape is inextricably linked with social value.

In 'Chaos in Motion and Not in Motion' (CP 357–8) Stevens begins by considering the arrangement of nature through painting and then goes on to consider the larger structure of the theatre in which an opera is being performed. The opening distich refers to the German painter, Ludwig Richter, and also identifies the conflict central to the poem – between the 'lashing wind' (the force of nature) and the spirit of the painter who would represent it in his pictures. As has been remarked, Stevens treats Richter ironically in this poem.[3] Indeed he is something of a soft target. Of this era of German art, it has been observed:

The high ideals of the Romantic were soon discarded. Their world-embracing emotions were replaced by a more personalized, intimate happiness, and the large-scale view of nature was transformed into a contemplative idyll. The past, the world of fairy-tales and pious legends, provided an escape from the miseries of the present and artists were inspired by sweet dreams of fairies, dwarfs, saints and princes. These attitudes were expressed by Ludwig Richter and Moritz von Schwind, whose works presented a happy, peaceful picture of life. (Lindemann 159)

Richter's paintings show humanity in harmony with nature. However, in Stevens's poem, this happy world, as Chris Beyers comments, is engulfed in a 'change and [a] decidedly unRichterian disorder, beginning with a July thunderstorm – a natural violence that would seem to imply an indifference for, or even a malevolence towards, humanity' (202):

> People fall out of windows, trees tumble down,
> Summer is changed to winter, the young grow old,
>
> The air is full of children, statues, roofs
> And snow.

Richter's *Storm*, which hangs in the National Gallery in Frankfurt-am-Main, with its innocent bucolic atmosphere, has no place for the representation of such a deluge of change. In that painting, we can see the familiar landscape space of Claude and Poussin, but Richter's handling of figure and colour dispels any notions of the Classicist ideals of the earlier French masters. The figures are fairy-tale caricatures; the colours are bright and varied, even cheerful in the face of the storm overhead. Richter so obviously fetishises nature that Stevens found in him a figure to suit his ironic purpose. The German painter's representation of nature is such confectionery that it takes only a wishful sigh to make it collapse: 'Oh, that this lashing wind was something more / Than the spirit of Ludwig Richter. . .'. However, before this wish is fulfilled, Stevens goes on to describe Richter's representation of the world in the following four distichs. He talks of it in the terms of opera, and it is worth noting that the fabulous tales that Richter took as his themes were often the subject of German opera in the nineteenth century (Abraham 456–7). Ludwig Richter's spirit comes to stand for the cultural production of a particular age – literature, music and, incorporating these three as a kind of *Gesamtkunstwerk*, opera. We see how Richter's landscape is part of the way in which a particular culture represented its world. And now the theatre, the building in which all these different arts are brought together, loses its hold on the ground (blown skywards by the wishful 'Oh' which opens the poem), and goes spinning through the air. In 'Repetitions of a Young Captain' (CP 306) we also find the image of the theatre overwhelmed by the elements:

> A tempest cracked on the theatre. Quickly,
> The wind beat in the roof and half the walls.
> The ruin stood still in an external world.

It is also the subject of the sixth and pivotal canto of 'The Auroras of Autumn' ('It is a theatre floating through the clouds'). The theatre, as one of the most important sites of cultural production, the place in which a society can represent to itself the world in which it lives, is uprooted and engulfed by the elements of nature. In 'Anecdote of Canna' the Capitol held together because the President was a figure of capable imagination. However, here nature breaks violently through the brittle representations of the schlemiel (Yiddish for 'loser'), Richter. It has no human focus and 'lashes everything at once': 'The theatre is spinning round, / Colliding with deaf-mute churches and optical trains'. As Richter's entire culture goes spinning off, his depictions of landscape have lost the whole in which they were contained. His canvas of the *Storm* breaks up and behind it a more frightening storm emerges, frightening for its inhuman aimlessness, for the indiscriminate force that has overwhelmed Richter's representation of it. It is the same fear that the scholar of one candle encounters when he walks out of his house in flames to confront the auroras as they move magisterially beyond all his representations and structures of knowledge.

The final distich of 'Chaos in Motion', which leaves us with the image of the wind, the vehicle of the simile, refuses to run smoothly on from Richter, operatic tenor to the earlier sopranos. We have the sense, not that Stevens is moving away from the scene to find a fitting vehicle with which to describe Richter, but is instead showing how Richter's will is dissolved within the scene around him. It is a failed metaphor, and the failure is expertly measured by Stevens. The enclosure that once served to protect the inhabitants from the elements is abandoned or destroyed and the forces of nature must be faced once more. The distich, its contents mirroring the first, presents us with the landscape's revenge on the fairy-tale landscape painter. Richter, who once arranged nature on his canvas, is lost in it.[4]

But those who limit their experience of landscape by 'rejecting' and 'denying' are not only 'floribund ascetics': on one occasion, as I pointed out earlier, Stevens takes the figure of Lenin and characterises him as a political leader precisely by the way that he organises and excludes certain elements of a lacustrine landscape (CP 343). On another, discussing a conversation between other revolutionaries, he portrays the fanaticism of one by the way he cannot perceive the landscape, the physical world that is surrounding him (CP 324–5).

> Victor Serge said, 'I followed his argument
> With the blank uneasiness which one might feel
> In the presence of a logical lunatic.'
> He said it of Konstantinov. Revolution
> Is the affair of logical lunatics [. . .]
>
> Lakes are more reasonable than oceans. Hence,
> A promenade amid the grandeurs of the mind,
> By a lake, with clouds like lights among great tombs,
> Gives one a blank uneasiness, as if
> One might meet Konstantinov, who would interrupt
> With his lunacy. He would not be aware of the lake.

He would be the lunatic of one idea
In a world of ideas, who would have all the people
Live, work, suffer and die in that idea
In a world of ideas. He would not be aware of the clouds,
Lighting the martyrs of logic with white fire.
His extreme of logic would be illogical.

The thrust of the passage is that it is reasonable to expect that Konstantinov would not be able to maintain the integrity of his idea when faced with the sea (unlike the doctor of Geneva [CP 24]), but he should at least be able to look at a lake.[5] However Konstantinov cannot, and he must 'reject' the lake, suppress it from his perception. What follows directly in 'Esthétique du Mal' is the much-quoted passage 'The greatest poverty is not to live / In a physical world'. Referring to this final section of the poem in her essay on Stevens and landscape, Bonnie Costello remarks: 'Stevens suggests not only that creation overwhelms human capability, that the physical absorbs the metaphysical, but that our "supreme fictions," our metaphysical inventions, learn their changes less from autonomous compositional laws than from physical surroundings' ('Adequacy' 216). In this section of 'Esthétique du Mal', however, Stevens is making a recommendation rather than stating a universal truth: our 'supreme fictions' *should* learn their changes from their physical changes, but often do not, as in the case of Konstantinov.

This flux is present to the two figures of 'On the Road Home' (CP 203–4). There is no turn to politics in the poem, or to any wider public context, but in the conversation that passes between the figures we witness the difficulty of fixing landscape and nature in human speech. Stevens's awareness of discourse, not as something that transparently represents the natural scene but as an agency in the midst of it, is acute. The poem could be read as a prelude to 'The Latest Freed Man', which has garnered more critical attention and follows it in the *Collected Poems*. It is a calm, difficult meditation about the landscape, and its calmness gives a dramatic abruptness to the opening lines of 'The Latest Freed Man' ('Tired of the old descriptions [. . .]'). However, one important point that the poems have in common is the way they construct themselves around the relationship between quoted speech and the rest of the poem. In the first, it is blatant as the reader tries to elucidate the connections. In the first verse, the general philosophical statement ('There is no such thing as the truth') collides with the particulars of the surrounding landscape, and it is in the phases of the difference between this discourse and the immediate natural world that the poem generates itself. (One is reminded of the first line of 'Questions Are Remarks' [CP 462]: 'In the weed of summer comes this green sprout why.') The general statement is tested against the particulars of the scene. The former does not impose its truth and erase all difference. Landscape is shown to be the site where fictions are most forcefully questioned rather than a touchstone of stability and order. Stevens, as we shall see as we go further in to this poem, valorises uncertainty and the conflict of interpretations when facing the landscape, playing this off against the philosophical discourse that would arrange and demarcate it.

There is a strong implication of causal connection between the utterance of the statement 'There is no such thing as the truth' and the grapes appearing fatter, and, although the second sentence is separated from the first by a full stop, the rhythm takes one past this barrier when the poem is read aloud, even when one gives adequate pause, and thus one considers the emerging fox as another effect of the utterance. In most of Stevens's work what is hardest to judge is how far he is being ironic: here, philosophical words, with startling immediacy, seem to change the world. Is Stevens ironising the idea that philosophy can change our world? If so, then we must take the finale, with its reported moment of imaginative plenitude, as ironic also: 'It was at that time, that the silence was largest / And longest, the night was roundest [...]'. The tone of these lines brings the poem to its rhetorical climax and seems devoid of irony. And yet if the poem is not then ironic at its finish, how can it have shifted tone so quickly in only fifteen lines?

Let us go through the poem again, this time giving more careful consideration to the relationship of the quoted speech to the rest of the text. In the first verse, the first person denies the existence of a single truth and that stance gives release to elements in nature: these are no longer suppressed by having to conform to a single idea. But what is also possible is that it is the awareness of this first person that is extended by his own uttered denial. He would not have remarked the grapes and the fox had he not made his declaration. In the next verse, the second person qualifies the first's statement by asserting a diversity of truths that do not integrate into a single truth. Again, this further denial, strengthened by the qualification, releases the narrator's awareness of his natural surroundings even further. The tree, we are told, does not *seem* to change, it actually begins to change – but at night, when it cannot be seen. What is important here, as the two figures in the wood successively deny a unitary truth, is that their awareness of their environment begins to broaden, unfolding outward, ever more open, until it is ready for that last culminating moment. The words they speak transform the landscape that they perceive. By this interpretation the poem does not glibly ironise the idea that philosophical thought changes the world, but defends it. With the further declaration of the fourth and fifth verses, the poem reaches its final moment of plenitude, which the two feel to be the zenith of their awareness of their surroundings, or at least so it is reported by the poem's narrator. In the fourth verse, we are given a statement that is homologous to the previous one concerning truth:

Words are not forms of a single word.
In the sum of the parts, there are only the parts.

The previously uttered words and their effect on the awareness of the two in the wood are reflected upon. It is as though the first person is kicking away the ladder – the words – that expanded his awareness. The climactic moment is reported by the first person as an event in retrospect, and the implication is that this moment when 'the silence was largest [. . .]' *was* shared by the other person, but this is by no means certain. The words uttered might not have induced a similar of extended awareness of the immediate natural environment. They might not have had a singularity of effect, just as 'Words are not forms of a single word.' The moment created by their utterance has, in this instance, two parts, two auditors, two parts of a world they share (and we recall that the poem is from the collection *Parts of a World*).

The two people, standing in a wood, are trying to negotiate their position in relation to the natural world that surrounds them, and, to a more subtle extent, to each other. The negotiation is complex, ambiguous and inconclusive. 'The world must be measured by eye', the first speaker declares. The world of the forest, the road, the fox in the hole, must be measured through the perception of the individual, through his perception and hermeneutic propensities, no matter to what uncertainties and complexities this leads. Just as all the matters of aesthetic beauty, poetry and society are to be worked out by the figure at the end of 'Imagination as Value' that I referred to in Chapter One, the one who is sitting in a public garden beside a statue. What is the land and what is nature that they can be changed or seem to change with uttered words? And if this question is difficult to answer, then how much more uncertain is the hypostasis of a politics, or a nationalism that would found itself on such images? A poem like this does not engage any one 'truth' and polemicise with it in the way that Jeffers's poems do. The excitement in and of this poem comes from the way different truths, different interpretations of the landscape, change, how they struggle for mastery, how our awareness of our natural surroundings can be transformed – enlarged or contracted – by a simple flick that adds to what is real and its vocabulary, to paraphrase 'Prologues to What is Possible' (CP 517).

To return then to the transition from Section XIV to XV of 'Esthétique du Mal', we see that Stevens does not thus avoid the political by taking landscape as his content: the political is also engaged, but only as one more 'fiction-genre' among others. Strangely, we may adduce Frank Lentricchia's essay again. In his analysis of 'O Florida, Venereal Soil' he points out how Stevens's treatment of the ethnic minorities in the poem makes it part of 'a modern lyric poetry [. . .] that could not successfully suppress the lost social ground of its emergence and its despair of social relation in America' (*Modernist Quartet* 146). The assumption here is that Stevens wanted to be Emerson, wanted to forget social contexts in the midst of nature, but this is inaccurate. Insofar as Stevens revered the moment of exaltation in nature (the same one that Emerson hymned at the beginning of *Nature*), Lentricchia is correct; but evident throughout the poetry is Stevens's desire to relate such moments to wider public contexts. Granted it is not often that this desire encompasses a discussion of particular social phenomena (such as émigrés in the US), but it is more accurate to see a poem like 'O Florida' against the backdrop of Stevens's lifelong meditation on the relations between the categories of the imaginative and the political.

Konstantinov does not live in a physical world but the ultimate politician can hear the words of the storm and of the people (CP 336); the latter does not need to 'reject' and 'deny' certain elements of his environment in order to bring into effect his political ideas. A better politics, better than that of Konstantinov and even of Serge, would show us how to live in the hermeneutic flux of the physical world. Of course, Stevens never specifies what that politics might be (although we can be sure it is not Marxist). He remains on the level of abstraction through-out. From one angle, this might seem analogous to the people in bars who always know what is wrong with a particular political set-up, but always stop short of putting themselves forward as candidates in elections. What does it mean to say that a good politics would be cognisant of the polyvalency of nature, would be aware that talk of 'noble' eagles is a category mistake? The move is primarily critical and not constructive, ironising the totalising space of classical and romantic landscape, as Costello put it ('Adequacy' 211), but also as a result the enclosing spaces of ideologies, be they national or Marxist which attempt to reject and deny the interpretive possibilities in the land. As I shall show in a reading of 'The Auroras of Autumn', Stevens does provide visions of détente between communities and the natural world, but even at these moments he does not go into political specifics. Nature then for Stevens does not come forward as solid hypostasis for social constructions, but rather as an interrogating and desta-bilising presence, dissolving the bonds which particular ideologies forge between communities and the land. In this, once again, the poetry plays the same role as most theory. The latter constantly produces insight into culture and society, but beyond gesturing to the vaguest of leftist utopias rarely suggests viable alternatives. To take just one example, David Harvey in *Justice, Nature and the Geography of Difference,* after a long and persuasive analysis of the relations between capital and geography, ends with the startlingly simplistic statement that we must somehow re-enchant our awareness of nature in order to counter-attack the ravages of global finance. This in no way invalidates his preceding analysis: we shall always have a need for writers who can provide synthesising overviews of the relations between societies and nature, or indeed of any large subject. On the most basic of levels, they help us understand the world, even if we refuse to act on their final recommendations. In another context altogether, when Seamus Heaney used the backdrop of the bog and the sacrificial victims it preserved for centuries as a way to understand the Troubles in Northern Ireland, he was accused by one critic of tacitly condoning the situation and not offering new ways of thinking about it (Carson 184–5). What the critic missed is that Heaney's poems in *North* (1975) provided the Irish community with the imagi-native equipment to think beyond the journalistic narrative of events; what was subsequently done after such possibilities are opened up becomes the responsibility of the people.

3

In my reading of 'How to Live. What to Do' at the end of the last chapter I stressed the connections the poem makes between the exaltation experienced in nature and the ethical concerns implicit in the title. Of course some readers might hear irony in the title (which recalls Nikolai Chernyshevsky's *What to Do?* [1863]), and thus think that Stevens, at least in this poem, is bidding social concerns farewell in favour of the aesthetic consolations of landscape. James Longenbach, for instance, says that the poem is a dramatisation of 'the private self's victory over public adversity' (131). I would counter by saying that more important than the putative irony in the poem is the speaker's location between an exalted awareness of landscape and public concerns. These are the important poles of the imagination in this poem and many others. What I wish to do in the readings that follow is show how Stevens moves between the poles of 'How to Live. What to Do', as he returns again and again to the natural world as the site of revelation of social meaning. I should remark here that it is not all about exaltation in nature: there are often moments of despair and weakness; but these are part of cycles of emotions that Stevens repeatedly connected with the cycle of the seasons, the despondency of winter followed by the exultation and plenitude of summer, and so on. These for him are fundamental to human thought and we have learnt our emotions from the weather: it is then not a symbol, as neither are the mountains, the sea, the sky, the trees, the flowers in bloom.

In 'Dry Loaf' (CP 199–200) Stevens's sense of how the arrangements of land-scape are connected with social formations is acute. And yet, as I have argued above, his representation of nature is not in the service of any particular ideology. It is polyvalent and frustrates attempts to employ the landscape scene as validation of some particular hegemony. Rather, social powers enter the arena of the landscape and suddenly discover the ground to be treacherous. They are afloat in hermeneutic uncertainty. This is what has been missed by previous critics of Stevens, the role that the natural world plays in meditations on the political and human history in general. The speaker of the poem is recounting a previous attempt of his to arrange the landscape as a background for his painting of the loaf of bread. One thinks immediately of those landscapes in Renaissance paintings that seem bleached of historical particularity (whether by the artist or the passage of time), serving only as featureless plain to set off the main object of interest (a person, a still-life arrangement). While he doesn't wish to present a sylvan idyll (we are told the people live in hovels), he is intent on some version of the picturesque, in the sense that the poverty in Breughel's paintings can be picturesque. But then the landscape starts to go out of control. It gathers a motive force surpassing that of his organising brush. The poem continues, picking up again on the image of the 'Birds that came like dirty water in waves [. . .]' In the next verse the repressed returns in gala panoply and the painter, another well dressed man with a beard, is utterly vanquished. Mention of the asphalt in this verse is particularly surprising as it locates the poem in the contemporary world whereas before it seemed as though a Renaissance painter was speaking. This reveals that the painter was deliberately trying to be anachronistic in his representation of nature, and erase all marks of the contemporary in favour of a timeless sylvan idyll. But the contemporary returns to trample on his aspirations:

> It was soldiers went marching over the rocks
> And still the birds came, came in watery flocks,
> Because it was spring and the birds had to come.
> No doubt that the soldiers had to be marching
> And that drums had to be rolling, rolling, rolling.

It is the sigh of resignation in the last two lines here that endear the speaker to us more than the well-dressed man with a beard. While his equation of the necessity of the birds' return with that of the soldiers is humorous, it takes an ominous turn with the last words of the poem ('rolling, rolling, rolling'): his humour and his painting will evaporate in the emergencies and alarms of war.

What is also of note here is the conflation of landscape with the social formation of the army. The equation of birds and soldiers is not completely serious, but demonstrates a need to understand the action of armies against nature. Also noteworthy is the fact that the eruption of the drums and soldiers into the sylvan idyll does not augur some kind of social realist allegory of landscape. The world of the soldiers, the birds and the mountains that we are left with at the end of the poem is curiously afloat and uncertain. The land is released into polyvalency after the speaker's attempts to restrict its symbolism. Thus, the poem records not only the speaker's failure to impress his meaning on the landscape but also that of the soldiers who are caught up in huge waves of birds and rocks. It is this overpowering rhythm of nature that the poem ultimately celebrates.

'Idiom of the Hero' (CP 200–1), which follows it immediately in the *Collected Poems*, would seem to turn all this on its head. The speaker here rejects social concerns in favour of skyscapes 'By which at least I am befriended'. But what Stevens is really rejecting here is crude configurations of the political: anybody who thinks that social chaos will soon be mended, as many figures on Left did in the US in the 1930s, deserves our ridicule. Stevens enjoins us to find better ways of thinking about the relations between skyscapes and politics.

This trajectory from land- and skyscapes to social relations is taken by 'Like Decorations in a Nigger Cemetery' (CP 150–8). The penultimate section of this poem goes like this:

XLIX

It needed the heavy nights of drenching weather
To make him return to people, to find among them
Whatever it was that he found in their absence,
A pleasure, an indulgence, an infatuation.

And then the last section:

L

Union of the weakest develops strength
Not wisdom. Can all men, together, avenge
One of the leaves that have fallen in autumn?
But the wise man avenges by building his city in snow.

This is the same kind of dismissal of the left that would resurface again in 'Idiom of the Hero' but it is not a dismissal of the political in toto.[6] It demands the answerability of social structures to the natural world, the kind of answerability that Marxism and certain forms of Capitalism can never provide because for them the natural world is primarily a resource, whether for industry or tourism. The city built in the snow will melt in springtime and then have to be rebuilt the following autumn: such a dismantling and reconstruction of social forms in concert with the seasons might on one level be also deserving of our ridicule but on another demand our respect. For this says that all human fictions – cities, paintings, poems – eventually fail and we would do as well to anticipate such failure in their design (the city of snow I take here to be a symbol, unlike the 'ever jubilant weather' with which I began this chapter).

The body of the poem, set out in haiku-like observations, which precedes these conclusions is brimming over with rich meditations on the relations between society and landscape. It is not considered one of his more important, which may not be because it doesn't have the sustained rhetoric of poems like 'The Auroras of Autumn' or 'Sunday Morning': its tone jumps from the arch to the impassioned to that of the measured observations above. (It could also be simply because of the distasteful title.) But there are treasures here, for instance in the humour that flashes out occasionally:

XLIII

It is curious that the density of life
On a given plane is ascertainable
By dividing the number of legs one sees by two.
At least the number of people may thus be fixed.

The first three lines would be enough in themselves, but the fourth, with its pursing of lips and mordant second thought, is highly comic. The poem is also full of tiny but intense exaltations and bright moments of plenitude:

II

Sigh for me, night-wind, in the noisy leaves of the oak.
I am tired. Sleep for me, heaven over the hill.
Shout for me, loudly and loudly, joyful sun, when you rise.

. . . .

XXVI

This fat pistache of Belgian grapes exceeds
The total gala of auburn aureoles.
Cochon! Master, the grapes are here and now.

. . . .

XXXI

A teeming millpond or a furious mind.
Gray grasses rolling windily away
And bristling thorn-trees spinning on the bank.
The actual is a deft beneficence.

The 'loudly and loudly' is the kind of exclamation we would expect more from
an exuberant Whitman, who is invoked in the preceding section, not Stevens.
And the abuse thrown at the Old Master is a more ebullient form of the
disapproval for the speaker of 'Dry Loaf': 'You pig! Look at the land and its fruits
before your very eyes, not those of Belgium!' And then the calm, clear beauty of
'The actual is a deft beneficence'. These are the declamations of a mind exulting
in the natural world 'from sheer Gemütlichkeit' (CP 152); these are the pleasures,
indulgences and infatuations (referred to in Section XLIX) that must be com-
prehended as the poem progresses.

Again and again in Stevens we read expressions of this simple, huge joy in
physical things, in having a body, in tasting fruit, looking at flowers, in air and
light, and not enough attention has been given to them. It is wrong to ignore
these moments in favour either of talk about Imagination and Reality or
demonstrations of how Stevens was imbricated in his times. It is not that such
characterisations are false, just that they are incomplete. They ignore the base
from which all Stevens's thought springs: the joys and despairs of being in
nature. The penultimate section that I quoted above gives the impression that
the return to society only occurs at the end of the poem, whereas it's present all
along. Early in the poem there is this instruction:

XV

Serve the rouged fruits in early snow.
They resemble a page of Toulet
Read in the ruins of a new society,
Furtively, by candle and out of need.

Paul-Jean Toulet's poetry did not have the optimistic Marxist exuberance of an Éluard: ironic, bitter, using condensed forms like those of 'Like Decorations', Toulet (1867–1920) is the voice of decadence when read in a new forward-looking socialist society. Here Stevens criticises the mind-numbing aspect of Marxist aspiration: it is simply tedious to talk of bright futures all the time. We also need decadence, irony, the expression of loss. This critique springs from a consideration of the rouged fruits against the backdrop of the cold season. Our relish for the fruits is the same as that for alternatives to monomaniac political systems.

But as Section XLIX points out, this is not just a case of analogy (fruits = Toulet; cold land = socialist society). The one who returns to the people has to find among them the *same* pleasures, indulgences and infatuations as he found in nature. He must not lose sight of the exaltations and intensity of vision that he experienced in the midst of the landscape. Those exaltations are sponsored by his awareness of the polyvalence of the natural world. The *cochon*-master is instructed to look at the grapes before his very eyes, but once facing nature in this immediate way we realise that new visions begin to blossom, not wither away. Stevens is writing a new kind sublime, one that reveals nature as polyvalent, the ground from which many different interpretive possibilities spring, and these have implications for the way communities figure themselves in their cultural works. This, after all, is what is being worked out in the poem. The figure of the artist/politician who moves from nature to society is one who will contribute to such cultural work, will offer his community representations of itself. When comparing Stevens's poetry with Jeffers's, I commented that for the latter nature is monovalent whereas Stevens's treatment of landscape and objects taken from nature reveals their interpretive abundance. Nowhere could this be more true that in 'Like Decorations in a Nigger Cemetery' where the variety of tone and attack from one section to the next enacts this polyvalency. And good cultural work, like good politics as we saw in the criticism of Konstantinov and Serge, will not suppress that polyvalency, but revel in it. When we examine this polyvalency of nature in the context of criticism of the Romantic sublime such as Jerome McGann's, we see that Stevens's poetry, instead of being indicted by such ideological critique, pushes it further in its considerations of society and its relationship to the world around it. This is what I wish to do in the next chapter.

Chapter 3

Public poetry and 'The Auroras of Autumn'

It will be because, though small
As measured against the All,
I have been so instinctively thorough
About my crevice and burrow.

– Robert Frost, 'A Drumlin Woodchuck'

Spread outward. Crack the round dome. Break through.

– 'Things of August'

1

The 'rejecting' and 'denying' that I discussed in Chapter Two are fundamental parts of the hermeneutic act: you must choose some things and exclude others in order to interpret. The critical climate of the last thirty years or so insists on the importance of what is *excluded* in the interpretive acts we find in literature and the arts. For instance, in the criticism of landscape painting there have been books investigating what has been called 'the dark side' of landscape: representations of the working classes were excluded from the picturesque view making landscape representation a discourse of imperialism deployed in order to naturalise its values. W. J. T. Mitchell, in his essay, 'Imperial Landscape', writes:

> Landscape might be seen more profitably as something like the 'dreamwork' of imperialism, unfolding its own movement in time and space from a central point of origin and folding back on itself to disclose both utopian fantasies of the perfected imperial prospect and fractured images of unresolved ambivalence and unsuppressed resistance. (10)

The task of criticism, according to this view, then becomes one of drawing attention to these 'fractured images', and of considering these imperial prospects to see what was excluded, glossed over, made ob-scene, and restore them to critical awareness. In many different cultural fields this kind of work has been carried out as connections are sought out between decorative representations of the land and social and political formations.[1]

Fredric Jameson, as we saw in Chapter Two, considers that Stevens laundered his landscapes of their social and cultural semantics. I showed how this statement is challenged by reference to certain poems; but nevertheless there is truth in what Jameson says insofar as Stevens takes on such themes as the interpretive act itself, thus becoming a focus for critical theory in the following decades. Frank Lentricchia has shown how Stevens was important for, among others, Frank Kermode in his *The Sense of an Ending: Studies in the Theory of Fiction* (1967), and how Stevens's poetry helped create a critical idiom, a way of talking about literature, which was widely current in American academe in the 1960s before the rise of Deconstruction (Lentricchia, *After the New Criticism* 34–5).

With these comments in mind, we must approach Stevens as a poet of nature and landscape in a different way from that prescribed by this tendency in criticism. Because Stevens took as one of his subjects the hermeneutic act itself – the process of excluding and denying – it is difficult to find a 'dark side' to his landscapes. Unlike the agents of the imperial prospect that Mitchell discusses in his essay, Stevens insists on the polyvalence of landscape and nature. Nature is the site where the monolithic interpretations of imperialism, in whatever form – be it a queen's or Lenin's or Nietzsche's ('Description without Place' [CP 339]) – are undone. In many poems he is aware of the valency that nature and landscape carry in political configurations: for instance, when sketching an idyllic pastoral scene he does not forget to remark who the ruler of the land is, since that fact changes our awareness of what we see. The problem for such 'dark side' critics of Romanticism is that Stevens is just as sophisticated, if not more so, in his theory as they are.

It is worthwhile for my discussion of Stevens to consider briefly McGann's powerful critique of the earlier Romantic poet, Wordsworth, not only because some of his remarks are of a piece with Jameson's, but also because the swerve to the left in the line of argument is typical of much contemporary criticism. In showing that such criticism is unhelpful as a way of approaching Stevens will enable me to demonstrate more precisely the kind of politics and configurations of the social we can find in Stevens's poetry. McGann analyses Romanticism, not, as he would say, by an uncritical acceptance of the parameters that Romantic works themselves provide, but rather by placing it in the very context that the 'Romantic ideology' wishes to repress in its cultural artefacts:

> The poetic response to the age's severe political and social dislocations was to reach for solutions in the realm of ideas. The maneuver follows upon a congruent Romantic procedure, which is to define human problems in ideal and spiritual terms. To characterize the Romantic Period as one marked by an 'epistemological crisis' is to follow Romanticism's own definition of its historical problems. (*Romantic Ideology* 71)

'The advantage of such a move, from the point of view of critical method', he continues, 'is that it supplies the critic with more ways for defining the special character of poetic works' (81). In theory, such an aim is wholly commendable, but problems arise in McGann's application of this approach to Romantic works. For instance, it leads him to contradiction in his reading of 'The Ruined Cottage': on one page he declares that 'Wordsworth is precisely interested in preventing – in actively countering' social and economic focuses in the poems, and yet on the facing page holds that this displacement is so effective that there is hardly any trace of this countering work that Wordsworth is alleged to be so fervently engaged upon (84–5). This is an unfair manoeuvre, since the burden of the proof lies with McGann to show where this active countering work is done in the poem. McGann is too subtle a critic to presume that poems should always discourse on the political, and thus accuse Wordsworth of retreating to a poetry of nature and consciousness. In his reading of Wordsworth's 'Tintern Abbey' he holds that the poem directly refers to unpleasant social realities connected with the place (the haunt of social outcasts) and the time (the anniversary of Bastille day), but notes that these are 'erased' in order for the poem to achieve its resolution (86).

Yet there is an underlying sense in his book that such a manoeuvre on Wordsworth's part is somewhat 'escapist'. For instance in the paragraph quoted above the implication seems to be that 'human problems' are so etherialised by their transfer to 'ideal and spiritual terms' that they cease to be 'human': it is, McGann holds, 'the deepest and most piteous loss' (88); the same presumption of 'loss' underlies Jameson's essay on Stevens. McGann states that the Romantic manoeuvre of resolving social and political contradiction in 'ideal and spiritual' planes (a kind of wishful thinking) involves 'the emergence of the concepts of Romantic Nature and Imagination as touchstones of stability and order' (67). These hypostases vouchsafe the poems' resolutions. It is not my intention to examine the interpretive force of this analysis in relation to Wordsworth and other poets of that era, but rather I adduce it to show more precisely how Stevens is working more subtly and more intelligently in his connections between the space of nature and that of politics. Willard Spiegelman, writing about the Romantic pastoral tradition in reply to some of the criticisms above, comments:

> Pastoral has never been, of course, quite so simple, and its habits of incor-porating criticism of both a political and a self-consciously literary sort have allowed it the amplitude to *seem* narrow and artificial while at the same time developing a resilient capacity to contain and reflect whatever its readers and critics wish to define as the chief qualities of literature itself. (110)

Stevens is, as is generally agreed, an inheritor and transformer of the Romantic tradition, but yet the concept of nature and the imagination's interviews with it are far from being 'touchstones of stability and order' that provide respite from political and social concerns: for him to go into nature is to precipitate interrogations of the dreamworks of imperialism which would restrict our awareness of the land and sky.

The problem that Stevens presents to 'dark side' critics is that his poetry theorises such exclusions. This concern with the hermeneutic act itself has long been seen by critics of his poetry as the dialectic of reality and the imagination. I do not wish to overthrow this idea entirely, but insist on qualifying the term 'reality', which, as Nabokov commented, is 'one of the few words which mean nothing without quotes' (312). The word 'reality' conjures up the vision of a Cartesian expanse of objects that are, in Coleridge's phrase, 'fixed and dead', and conveys no idea whatsoever of this world possessing a troping force. Nature throws forth 'forms, flames, and the flakes of flames'. The poet must face these auroral transformations and ask what they are, what caused them and how the troping force of his own imagination relates to them. However, as he moves from *Harmonium* into the work of the 1930s, Stevens becomes aware of how ideological formations condition and sometimes restrict our apprehension of these forms and flames, and his theme becomes the phases of the difference between the impoverishing dreamworks of imperialism and a nature fecund with so many selves and sensuous worlds.

In this chapter and the next I want to look closer at how this dynamic of enclosure and open horizon works in Stevens's poetry. As we shall see, some of the enclosures that Stevens also leaves behind him are those of previous Romantic correspondences in nature, fixed tableaux, douce campagnas, as well as the arrogant reading of nature as simply a text of human emotions. Stevens's poems work to restitute the hermeneutic complexity of the interview of humanity and nature, and thus the moment of leaving these various enclosures is significant since it is also the moment when he leaves behind the erasures and suppressions of previous readings of nature. I shall show how Stevens, far from rehearsing these ideas as solitary agon, figures them as the quest of a community, a congregation in the wilderness. This will lead me to a more in-depth consideration of the sense in which we can say that Stevens's characterisations of communities and nature is political. Here I shall argue that 'The Auroras of Autumn', even while it avoids specific contemporaneous political concerns and cannot be read back into its historical moment, provides a ceremonious rhetoric that provides a community with a vision of its place in the world. Prior and necessary to all political and ideological thought must be this sense of a community's shared fate and its place on the earth. Such work is usually done by mythology and religion, but Stevens's poem is remarkable for its acute sense of the way that this mythopoesis is constantly active around us, creating the time and place in which we breathe, so that for him mythology and ideology blend together, or happen simultaneously.

Investigating the relationship between poetry and philosophy in his essay 'A Collect of Philosophy' Stevens opens with a quotation from Bruno, the 'orator of the Copernican theory':

> By this knowledge we are loosened from the chains of a most narrow dungeon, and set a liberty to rove in a more august empire; we are removed from presumptuous boundaries and poverty to the innumerable riches of an infinite space, of so worthy a field, and of such beautiful worlds . . . (OP 267)

Bruno goes on to assert that every part of this newly perceived universe harmonises with the divine beauty and that '[t]here is but one celestial expanse, where the stars quire forth unbroken harmony'. The point that Stevens draws from this is that while it is sixteenth-century philosophy it is also sixteenth-century poetry, and it allows us to understand Victor Hugo's statement that 'the stars are no longer mentionable in poetry'. In turn, I wish to draw a point from Stevens's point: although Stevens, through Hugo, remarks on the way that this sixteenth-century poetic imagery and its philosophy are no longer viable, there is still something here in Bruno's description of the Copernican moment that is central to Stevens's own poetry, and indeed to that of many other poets, that is, the moment of change, release from enclosure into an apparently unlimited realm of possibility. For Bruno this realm is cosmic in its proportions; for Stevens the scale is reduced – landscapes are the places where these changes occur. Nevertheless, the change is no less momentous. Bruno's figure is a prisoner in a dungeon who is released from his physical confines and experiences the boundlessness of cosmic space. Stevens's figures are various, but the *volte* of some of his most important poems occur about the realisation that the enclosures that limit the awareness of landscape and nature (through rejecting and denying certain elements, as we saw in the last chapter) can be surpassed, thus leading into uncertain hermeneutic zones. These zones are beyond those of conventional nature poetry, which present a fixed scene, a 'douce campagna', an ideology. This is, as I showed, one of the ways that Stevens differs from a poet like Jeffers. Sometimes this moment of access to the polyvalence of landscape is gained through the destruction of an exhausted imagery, for instance in the way 'Montrachet-le-Jardin' (CP 263) rejects the Classical scene of 'Terra Paradise' with its 'autumn rivers, silvas green, / [. . .] sanctimonious mountains high in snow' for the more factual landscape that he itemises at the poem's conclusion.

The problem of the rationalists which concludes 'Six Significant Landscapes' (CP 73–5) is that their enclosures, the rooms they live in, condition the way they think and they are thus incapable of dealing with the kind of ambiguity that landscapes, according to Stevens, create. Indeed what is noticeable about the sixth significant landscape of this poem is that there is no landscape at all.

Rationalists, wearing square hats,
Think, in square rooms,
Looking at the floor,
Looking at the ceiling.
They confine themselves
To right-angled triangles.
If they tried rhomboids,
Cones, waving lines, ellipses –
As, for example, the ellipse of the half-moon –
Rationalists would wear sombreros.

The punchline – the image of a university logician exchanging his mortarboard for the eccentric curves of a sombrero – is expertly timed. And contrary to what I said, we see that there is a hint at a landscape that the rationalists are ignoring: 'the ellipse of the half-moon'. But the rationalists, as figures of *in*capable imagination, ensconced in the rooms of their academies, are not able to face the hermeneutic uncertainties of nature and thus will never don sombreros. For instance, the figure of Section III of the poem comments that his eye is powerful, making him taller than any tree and allowing him to reach the shore of the sea. However, as he remarks wryly at the end, he dislikes 'The way the ants crawl / In and out of [his] shadow'. While he is powerful in a specular sense, he is compromised in another: the image of the ants moving in and out of his shadow shows him as vulnerable to the smallest creatures. Nevertheless, he is more capable than the rationalists since he faces the landscape and chooses not to take refuge in some enclosure that would cordon off such threats to his identity.

Stevens's poems sometimes present a choice between enclosure and open horizon, and his approbation is reserved for those figures who are able to brave the elements, brave the vision of auroral changes that nature presents and not be destroyed. In his later poetry he was concerned with the ways in which human communities can negotiate such episodes. This is a type of power, the power to be transformed (CP 514). These figures must be strong enough to undergo catharsis when facing nature and rise to the challenge offered them. What they learn has implications for the communities and societies they return to. Less courageous figures are castigated: for Herr Doktor of 'Delightful Evening', a precursor of the fastidious Professor Eucalyptus and a figure of incapable imagination, 'The twilight [is] overfull / Of wormy metaphors' (CP 162). He would scurry back to his room to avoid the squirming possibilities that the evening presents him with. He is the type who would opt for enclosure, plump for 'rejecting' and 'denying' certain parts of the landscape so that it is subordinated to his imaginative perception. Herr Doktor would like to be able to distort the twilight and accommodate it to his systematic *Weltanschauung*. In reading the following poems we shall leave the fearful Herr Doktor behind and look at those moments in the poetry when the enclosure is forgone to face the changes of nature. This will bring me to the matter of Stevens's relation to Frost, since, as Richard Poirier has pointed out, these issues of enclosure and open horizon are important also in the latter's work (*Robert Frost* 87ff). I shall show how both poets on some occasions think about nature in the same way and then I shall go on to show how they differ. Frost is considered the nature poet *par excellence* of his era, and comparing him with Stevens will enable me to show what kind of nature poet Stevens is not, and thus come nearer a description of the kind he is.

In several poems in the collection, *The Auroras of Autumn* (1950), we see this movement from enclosure to wider horizons. In Section II of 'Things of August' (CP 490) we are enclosed within an egg that, granted, does not completely exclude nature (we see the glittering of the Adirondacks and we smell the 'myrrh and camphor of summer'), but this is not enough. The poem, as it swiftly switches to the imperative, registers the impatience of the speaker with this enclosure that restricts his participation in the landscape:

Spread outward. Crack the round dome. Break through.
Have liberty not as the air within a grave

Or down a well. Breathe freedom, oh, my native,
In the space of horizons that neither love nor hate.

While inhabiting the egg, one supposes that those horizons were bent into 'pathetically false' shapes (that love and hate), and if the movement from enclosure to horizon in Stevens's poetry means anything it means that nature should not be read only as a text of our emotions. By breaking through we learn to behold 'Nothing that is not there and the nothing that is' (CP 10). This access to landscape and nature is not like gazing at a blank canvas upon which our emotions and thoughts must be projected, which is the way that Coleridge thought of it, as the imagination 'struggles to idealize and to unify', being 'essentially *vital*, even as all objects (as objects) are essentially fixed and dead' (Coleridge 167). (Stevens extensively marked his copy of I. A. Richards's *Coleridge on Imagination* [1934], and the latter's characterisation of Coleridge's attitude to nature [Richards 157–63] accords with the one I present here.) In Stevens, as we shall see, our deepest reserves of emotion and intellect are drawn upon; but instead of forcefully imposing the imagination's constructions on nature, we are called upon to perceive, to use our senses once again and test the old symbolisms, religions, mythologies against the contingencies of the weather, of the scene with tree, house and hill.

It is with such a scene that 'Evening without Angels' (CP 136–8) ends. In the way that the poem hinges on the extinction of the Christian mythology and its attendant angels it is, like some of Stevens's poems, a rewriting of Milton's 'On the Morning of Christ's Nativity' where the mythological figures of antiquity are ousted by the new born Jesus:

67

> The lonely mountains o'er,
> And the resounding shore,
>   A voice of weeping heard, and loud lament;
> From haunted spring, and dale
> Edged with poplar pale,
>   The parting genius is with sighing sent,
> With flower-inwoven tresses torn
> The nymphs in twilight shade of tangled thickets mourn.   (109)

However, the difference is that in Stevens's poem there is no similar substitute – the angels are no longer present and no new ones arrive: 'Air is air, / Its vacancy glitters round us everywhere'. Instead of some second coming, the advent of a rough beast that inaugurates a new age, we are left with the scene of the community in their houses gathered beneath the majestic changes sweeping through the sky, which prefigures the strong concern with images of community in the late phase of Stevens's career.

> Bare night is best. Bare earth is best. Bare, bare,
> Except for our own houses, huddled low
> Beneath the arches and their spangled air,
> Beneath the rhapsodies of fire and fire,
> Where the voice that is in us makes a true response,
> Where the voice that is great within us rises up,
> As we stand gazing at the rounded moon.

The four 'bare's in the first line here put up firm barriers against Yeats's kind of mythopoeia that would conjure the rough beasts of the new era, and the poem ends by constructing a landscape scene in which a détente is found between the community of the houses and the forces of nature. They do not impose their mythologies, they listen to 'the rhapsodies of fire and fire' that are moving through the sky and they answer these. '[T]he voice that is great within us rises up' because it is called by the weather: the community of the poem is responding to the contingencies of the natural world. When we come to 'The Auroras of Autumn' we shall see the elements of this scene – house, trees, weather, the community gathered beneath the elements (the trees, although not mentioned in the closing lines of 'Evening without Angels', appear in its opening lines) – amplified to produce one of Stevens's greatest poems. Richard Poirier has commented how such a scene is particularly American, employing 'images of housing, of possession, and of achieving by relinquishment of one's inheritance some original relation to time and space' (*World Elsewhere* 19). Exposure to the elements affirms strength and brings knowledge.

It is such an exposure that the 'lonely womenfolk' of Robert Frost's 'The Cocoon' fear (Frost 247–8). The community of 'Evening without Angels' know that they have spun their cocoon. But here the knowledge of the détente between the people and the landscape is restricted to the speaker of Frost's poem. The way the last line echoes the last but fourth conveys the poet's sympathy for these women who are 'inmates' in their house. What is not directly expressed in the poem (yet drives it on) is the inhabitants' fear of confronting the elements. Frost does not tell us of any dangerous beast or man circling the house. The fear they feel is more vague. The house provides them with a defence between what is too much and themselves, to paraphrase another poem (Frost 349). Frost does not need to express this fear openly since it is present in so many other poems that present similar scenes: purely by this force of association we know immediately what the women are afraid of. A few poems on in *West-Running Brook* (1928) the short poem, 'Lodging', expresses the idea almost aphoristically (Frost 250). It is humorous and yet clearly gestures to the life-threatening dangers of exposure to the open elements. Nevertheless, there are occasionally 'cocoons', which can be houses, the smoke coming out of houses, or, as we frequently find in Frost's work, poetic form itself. The smoke in 'The Cocoon' insofar as it is witnessed only by the poet echoes with the form of the poem itself that offers its 'stay against confusion'.

The divergence between Frost and the Stevens of 'Evening without Angels' is pronounced if we consider a poem like 'Desert Places'. Here Frost feels the loneliness that the women felt in 'The Cocoon'. The speaker is the only figure abroad in the twilight – even the 'animals are smothered in their lairs'. Both poets face the same 'bareness', but whereas Stevens was exhilarated by the evening air evacuated of angels and felt a voice that was great within the community rising up, Frost is 'scared' by the 'blanker whiteness of benighted snow / With no expression, nothing to express' (Frost 296).

> They cannot scare me with their empty spaces
> Between the stars – on stars where no human race is.
> I have it in me so much nearer home
> To scare myself with my own desert places. (Frost 296)

And yet it would be wrong to say Frost was fearful and Stevens courageous. The convergences and divergences between the two poets that I have sketched out here do not do justice to the mercurial qualities of Frost's poetry and to the way that he can change tack from poem to poem. The last stanza of 'Sand Dunes' in *West-Running Brook* is very close to the last section of 'Six Significant Landscapes' (Frost 260–1). My purpose in ranging these different poems by Frost around Stevens's 'Evening without Angels' is to see the preoccupations that the poets share. This scene with house and huge sky stretching above it – the interview between enclosure and open horizon – is where their imaginations work to find terms for themselves and communities when faced with the plastic force of nature; they find ways to maintain the integrity of their enclosures, the poetic forms within which they write. For Stevens this means asserting 'the voice that is great within us' in the face of the evening sky and often mocking those figures of incapable imagination such as Herr Doktor of 'Delightful Evening'. And for Frost it is changes of the speaker's mood from fearfulness to fearlessness.

A Frost poem that encapsulates the complexity of his position is 'There are Roughly Zones' (and it is worth remarking that the scene presented in the poem is almost identical to that of 'Evening without Angels'). The skies at the end of Stevens's poem seem to be preparing for a storm, and in 'There are Roughly Zones' it is the north-west wind that is now blowing with all its force upon the house. In the opening lines the poem gestures toward the kind of fearfulness of the 'lonely womenfolk' in 'The Cocoon', but quickly dismisses it.

> We sit indoors and talk of the cold outside.
> And every gust that gathers strength and heaves
> Is a threat to the house. But the house has long been tried.
> We think of the tree. (Frost 305)

It is the tree that must survive the storm. It might not leaf again since it is a peach tree, we are told, and might not be able to stand the northern climate to which it has been transplanted. The people are safe and although confined within the tried-and-tested house they are human beings who have enough ambition 'to extend the reach / Clear to the Arctic of every living kind'. And even if this ambition will prove to be the death of the peach tree, it echoes with the 'voice that is great within us' at the end of 'Evening without Angels'. Both poets find in the scene tropes of imaginative capability. While Stevens celebrates the harmony between the sky's rhapsodies and the human voice, Frost dwells on its deleterious effects. The consolation for the peach tree is that 'if it is destined never again to grow, / It can blame this limitless trait in the hearts of men' – Frost, tongue-in-cheek here, supposing the peach tree can blame. Instead of braving the elements themselves, they send a proxy to suffer in their place while they remain under roof. That these ambitious people whose hearts contain the 'limitless trait' (which evokes the more common phrase 'limitless tract' of land; 'trait' and 'tract' are also cognates) happen to be in the house wondering if the beams will hold against the wind is the source of the poem's complexity. Expanses are enclosed within small quarters. The huge sky rhymes with the 'limitless trait' inside the hearts of humans. There is no simple inside/outside opposition here. Humans, Frost tells us, possess a power comparable to nature's if they stay roughly within certain zones and obey those zones' rules, but when their Romantic arrogance pushes them to exceed these rules, Nature corrects it.

I would like to end this group of readings by turning to Stevens's parable of the people who remained in their houses and who, like those of 'There are Roughly Zones', have access to an imaginative power because of this. 'Wild Ducks, People and Distances' (CP 328–9) is an unobtrusive short poem tucked in before the more discussed 'Pure Good of Theory'. Though from later in Stevens's career, the poem's scene is the same as 'Evening without Angels' and, indeed, is a variation on that same theme. This time, however, no great voice is found to 'choir it with the naked wind' (CP 415). Also the poem, like the earlier 'Evening without Angels', employs the first person plural. The community of the poem has grown used 'so soon, too soon' to the elements in which it lives. But although they have become too accustomed to the scene, we are told in the opening lines that the life of the world depends upon these people in their villages, and the poem ends by reasserting their importance. Huge tensions are at work:

> It was that they were there
> That held the distances off: the villages
> Held off the final, fatal distances,
> Between us and the place in which we stood.

The menace that is quietly conveyed by the word 'fatal' is the same as that which we found in Frost. And again, as in Frost, we have the juxtaposition of enclosure with open horizon, the villages, with their 'weather of other lives' which cannot be escaped, and the fatal distances through which the ducks are flying. The scene is no static tableau but a balance of great torques and torsions.

Many critics have remarked how Frost's poems are often meditations on poetic form itself. As in 'The Cocoon', the scene in the poem can be one of house and landscape but we are constantly nudged by him to consider the poem we are reading as another type of house, a structure that holds out for a while against the greater troping force of nature. The strong deliberate rhymes played off against a deceptively colloquial voice also reproduce this interview of enclosure and open horizon. Frost himself felt that his work was full of literary criticism, by which we can suppose he meant theorising about the poetic act itself (see Poirier, *Robert Frost* xi). Poirier's study of Frost has shown how this type of theorising is central to a poetic oeuvre that we too often consider as merely nature poetry, a kind of noble pedestrian pursuit that has none of the intellectual dazzle of more philosophical poetry by someone like Stevens; the opposition is superficial. Frost's example is alluring as it shows how nature poetry can expound theories of poetry while still being about nature. Obviously with Stevens, the case is inverted: he is normally considered as the philosophical poet *par excellence* while Frost is, as I remarked earlier, that of nature. The balance between theory and nature that Poirier finds in Frost invites us to see the 'nature' in Stevens's work without losing sight of its 'theoretical' aspects, by which I mean not just complex meditations on reality and imagination, but also on the relations between the artwork and social formations. I show how Stevens worked again and again with nature, landscapes and weather, trees and flowers, not as props for some philosophical exposition (as Jameson holds), but as scenes that contain contingencies and forces whose relationship to the human act of 'making' (poems, towns, houses, polities, nations) must be continually renegotiated. In 'Wild Ducks' this is a system of enormous tensions, one thing depending on the other, holding the scene in place, like the relations between the two figures and nature in 'On the Road Home'. The natural world is not a prop for a voice producing endless variations on the same theme: it intrudes upon Stevens's philosophical exposition, interrupting it and continually forcing it to regroup, and making him reassess wider social contexts. Such an approach lets us see nature poetry not as something that excludes the 'theory of poetry' (which is necessarily a theorising of society also), but on the contrary becomes its greatest occasion. In Chapter Four I shall show how the horizon of nature helped Stevens think through the political concerns of the 1930s, aiding him in his meditations on the great masses of men that seem to crowd in on him and so many others in that decade. It is this kind dependence between natural scenes and such extensive theorising of poetry and the political that has heretofore been passed over by critics of Stevens.

Nevertheless, although we can agree that a similar balance exists in both poets' work between the demands of nature and theory, I do not wish to erase the differences. The fractious standoff between these two tropers in Florida is enough to indicate what a divide separated their work. 'Stevens said to Frost, "The trouble with you is you write about things." And Frost replied, "The trouble with you is you write about bric-a-brac"' (Brazeau 160). On another occasion Stevens commented that he just didn't like Frost's poetry (Brazeau 68). According to Mary Jarrell, Frost felt the divide very strongly also: '[There was] a deep, smoldering, incurable resentment that Frost had about Stevens. [It was partly the result] of Frost's acute sensitivity at being a nonintellectual poet, somebody [for] *Saturday Evening Post* readers or *Atlantic Monthly* readers, and Stevens being such an intellectual. Frost always divided the world into intellectuals and himself' (Brazeau 181; parentheses Brazeau's). We should qualify this by saying that Frost's acute sensitivity was probably at being *considered* a non-intellectual poet rather than at being one. Poirier's study shows that while most of his work could be comfortably digested by *Atlantic Monthly* readers, it was not read by them in all its imaginative complexity. Whether the source of this mutual dislike was personal or aesthetic, and even though we can admit that their works have points in common, reading a Frost poem is a very different experience to reading a Stevens poem. Though both poets often use 'we', Stevens invariably sounds vatic and Frost demotic. Stevens rarely employed rhyme while Frost often achieved startling effects through it. And most importantly there is a strong identification between Frost's speakers in the poems and Frost himself. Poirier writes that it is pedantic to differentiate these latter. Easily – and perhaps too easily – do readers make the connection between Frost's lyric voice and his public persona. Frost himself invites it. This means that despite all our expeditions with him to 'desert places' we are not deserted by this persona.

That such identification is very hard to make in Stevens's case is clear if we consider Peter Brazeau's oral biography of Stevens beside his *Collected Poems*.

We could never imagine the public Stevens of the former book speaking the way his poems do. From *Harmonium* onwards Stevens often throws his voice with the result that by the end of his career there is no one persona that anchors all the poems. Consequently, he is often thought of as an impersonal poet. (Helen Vendler, in *Words Chosen Out of Desire*, has shown how there are some very personal moments embedded in poems that are normally considered impersonal.) Of course, all the poems are distinctly his own, and yet by reading them alone we would have very little sense of what it would be like, say, to meet their author socially. On the one hand, this disjunction is enabling since it brings freedom; disabling, since the poetry's diction can lose some of its vitality when so removed from the public domain, which is, after all, its origin. But the way that Stevens uses this freedom, especially in the longer poems, is exhilarating. It allows him a range of reference that is impossible for Frost. This is not to say that it is not also exhilarating to see Frost achieve comparable effects within the confines of such a public poetry (and I mean 'public' in the sense of the last paragraph), but the distance of Stevens's language from that of his public persona allows him to let the language of philosophy and theory appear in work that is still, in essence, nature poetry. Stevens moves through the landscape with philosophic verve.

It is from such a position that I wish to read the long poem, 'The Auroras of Autumn' (CP 411–21). It is pivoted around the movement from enclosure to open horizon that occurs in Canto VI. This is the point of highest risk and most profound regeneration.

> He opens the door of his house
>
> On flames. The scholar of one candle sees
> An Arctic effulgence flaring on the frame
> Of everything he is. And he feels afraid.

But quoting these lines out of the context of the poem gives no idea of the freight they carry. Indeed reading 'The Auroras of Autumn' out of the context of the rest of Stevens's work gives no idea of the freight it carries either. Stephen Matterson has commented how

> [W]e need to understand Stevens's work by seeing it as a body of poetry; poems such as 'Earthy Anecdote' and 'The Planet on the Table' surely mean very little unless we refer them to Stevens's recurring themes. That is, he is not a lyric poet in the same way that Frost is.

Frost's poems are 'self-contained' and this 'helps to explain why *The Atlantic Monthly* accepts Frost [...] and would find Stevens incomprehensible' (Matterson). 'The Auroras of Autumn' is a dense meditation that is supported by the five collections of poetry that precede it, and, as Matterson goes on to comment, its

73

use of the sequence, as is so frequent in Stevens, is indicative once again of the difference of his approach with Frost's, whose momentary stays against confusion are much tighter enclosures than Stevens's more open forms.

Canto I sets the scene for the poem. It is a landscape. There is a search for 'the serpent', for the genius of the auroral changes sweeping through the sky. We must search for it among

> These fields, these hills, these tinted distances,
> And the pines above and along and beside the sea.

When we reach the cabin in Canto II we have a scene of house and landscape that is very similar to that of 'Evening without Angels'. Despite the changes that occur in the rest of the poem we are brought back in the last canto to the same image of a habitation, 'hall harridan', that stands beneath 'a haggling of wind and weather' (CP 421). Again it is enclosure and open horizon that forms the mise-en-scène against which everything takes place.

The questions that each successive canto of the poem attempts to answer is what are these lights moving through the sky? Are they 'a spell of light', a 'false sign', a 'saying out of a cloud' (CP 418)? What causes them? 'Is there an imagination that sits enthroned / As grim as it is benevolent' that takes 'its place in the north and enfold[s] itself'? 'And do these heavens adorn / And proclaim it' (CP 417)? In an attempt to answer these questions, Cantos I to VI provide an excursus through the mechanics of mythopoeia – the means by which humans situate themselves in nature and in relation to each other. Moving from the sinuous landscape of Canto I to the cosmic visions of Canto IV, we say 'Farewell to an idea . . .', as Stevens pushes each mythopoeic figuration to its limits to see how much it gives. The verb 'gives' here I use in three senses: how much it gives humanity in the sense of serving it; how much it bends to the pressure exerted upon it by the auroral changes sweeping across the sky; and, connected with this, how much it gives *onto* nature and the auroras. And these 'ideas', that of the mother of Canto III, the father on his throne in Canto IV, the raucous party of Canto V, all take place within the framing structure of the cabin/house introduced in Canto II and abandoned in Canto VI.

Having said farewell to the idea of the serpent of the opening canto we find ourselves in Canto II looking at a cabin standing 'Deserted, on a beach [. . .]'. What the first few lines try to answer is, 'why is the cabin white?' The same 'why' is directed at the auroras throughout the whole poem: 'why are they the way they are?' The question, asked of both the auroras and the cabin, allows Stevens to discover the difference between that which man makes and that which nature makes. '[T]he phases of this difference' (CP 420) between a people and their world are what will be explored in the final canto. One of these phases will be concerned with the question of whether humanity's imagination is the same as that of nature. Are they identical? If not, then what do they share? The whiteness that the flowers are trying to remind us of is compared with that of the sky, that which stretches 'from horizon to horizon'. The meditation on these different whitenesses is like Frost's 'Design' and the two pieces are similar also in terms of theme. They both ask who arranges the things that we see, and why. What is also worth remarking in the passage is Stevens's historical sense, as customs are passed from one generation to the next. I shall discuss his interest in the history of Pennsylvania and Connecticut in Chapter Five, but for now I wish to register that the figure who has constructed the cabin is no Adam sprung up unparented from the soil, but the latest in a long line of ancestors who have passed on to him their values and styles of building.

Whoever arranged and built the cabin is no longer here. We are told '[t]he wind is blowing sand across the floor'. Unlike 'Evening without Angels' there are no inhabitants who find a 'great voice' to choir with the auroral changes in the sky. The cabin stands as a reminder of how each 'human arrangement' is '[p]lace-bound and time-bound' (CP 363). '[T]he whiteness grows less vivid' and a life ends. Above this abandoned habitation

> the north is always enlarging the change,

> With its frigid brilliances, its blue-red sweeps
> And gusts of great enkindlings, its polar green,
> The color of ice and fire and solitude.

Whose solitude is this? Is it of the man who 'turns blankly on the sand'? Is it the solitude of the agent of the auroral changes, nature itself? That the man turns *blankly* aligns him with the whiteness of the cabin and its flowers. And this blankness is in contrast with the spectacular colours of this last tercet. Although the man observes the natural magnificence of the auroras, his presence, revealed at the end of the canto, does not console in the way that Frost's persona does. His voice does not keep the reader company during these moments of spiritual destitution.

As we move from the cabin to the mother's house to the father's feast of the following cantos we realise that these changes of tack from one canto to the next are an effort to follow the sublime metamorphoses that are occurring in the sky above the speaker. It is Odysseus' struggle to keep up with Proteus on the beach. As the house starts 'dissolving' in Canto III the figure of the mother is invoked as 'the purpose of the poem', an imaginative force that will hold things together beneath the enlarging changes in the sky. 'And yet she too is dissolved, she is destroyed' (CP 413).

The meditations on the cabin, house and theatre are the speaker's ways of inquiring how to situate himself in the midst of such huge natural changes. The solution must *give onto* the changes, it must not 'reject' and 'deny', like the fictions of the well-dressed man with a beard, in order to maintain its integrity. Crispin was able to build his cabin and that served to confine his vision of the continent, but here the changes of the auroras outstrip the speaker's attempt to represent them, or to find representational spaces to account for them. And although Canto IV, which could be a fabliau of scientific knowledge, comes closest to moving out into open space, it still has the father enthroned as director of a masque that futilely hopes to 'choir it with the naked wind'. That it is science (which 'measures the velocities of change') seen as a choiring masque is an attractive reading of this canto, but the dismissiveness of the rhetorical question with which it concludes indicates that the father's artifice obscures more than it reveals, that it does not give onto the auroral changes.

The father is 'enthroned', we are told at the end of the canto, and thus what started as a cabin is now a palace (could we be moving from Crispin to Hoon?). From here the jump is easy to the planet of VII. Each successive habitation is an attempt to live with the change, and the speaker is forced to enlarge the habitation to comprehend the auroras, an enclosure that is '[e]qual in living changingness to the light' (CP 380). Canto V draws the three ideas of the house, the mother and father together into a festival of human artifice: dance, music, theatre. We have '[s]cenes of the theatre, vistas and blocks of woods' but still we are enclosed: these are *maquettes* of nature, and we have no feeling of access to its huge ambiguous horizons through which the auroras disport themselves. We are still confined within pageants of human artifice that do not give onto the auroral changes moving over the landscape. Stevens's frustration is growing as he longs to escape the clauses and *claustra* of this house. The enclosure is stifling, human artifice is crowded in on itself – a window needs to be thrown open, a wall knocked out.

This mounting feeling of stiflement is released in the next canto in the frightening moment of the scholar walking out of the house in flames. The house has turned into the theatre that is engulfed by that which it wished to represent and control. For Nietzsche, this was the fundamental Dionysian moment when 'the Olympian magic mountain [. . .] opened up before us and revealed its roots' (Nietzsche 42). We feel '[t]hat overwhelming dismay in the face of the titanic powers of nature' (42). Its opposite, Apollonian culture, is seen in terms of an edifice. Hierarchy, order, morality are important to it (41). The Dionysian state, he says later on, implies 'the annihilation of the ordinary bounds and limits of existence' (59).

Stevens read Nietzsche as a young man and returned to him late in life (for a good discussion of this see Bates 241–65). *The Birth of Tragedy* (1872), from which these quotations are taken, is about the origins of Greek drama. Towards its conclusion, 'The Auroras' is concerned with tragic form as the way in which a community expresses its relation to the titanic forces of nature, and what it thinks of itself. (Later, in Canto IX, he talks of 'This drama that we live', as well as referring to *Hamlet* – 'We were as Danes in Denmark', etc.) We can connect it with Canto VI not only on a conceptual level but also in terms of imagery. In Section 8 of *The Birth of Tragedy*, Nietzsche propounds the idea that there was no distinction between the chorus and the audience in early Greek tragedy. The person watching the play can '*overlook* the whole world of culture around him and [. . .] imagine, in absorbed contemplation, that he himself was a chorist' (63). This fact, he holds, is connected with the shape of the theatre:

> The form of the Greek theater recalls a lonely valley in the mountains: the architecture of the scene appears like a luminous cloud formation that the Bacchants swarming over the mountains behold from a height – like the splendid frame in which the image of Dionysus is revealed to them. (63)

And here is Canto VI:

> It is a theatre floating through the clouds,
> Itself a cloud, although of misted rock
> And mountains running like water, wave on wave,
>
> Through waves of light. It is of cloud transformed
> To cloud transformed again, idly, the way
> A season changes color to no end,
>
> Except the lavishing of itself in change,
> As light changes yellow into gold and gold
> To its opal elements and fire's delight,
>
> Splashed widewise because it likes magnificence
> And the solemn pleasures of magnificent space.
> The cloud drifts idly through half-thought-of forms.
>
> The theatre is filled with flying birds,
> Wild wedges, as of a volcano's smoke, palm-eyed
> And vanishing, a web in a corridor
>
> Or massive portico. A capitol,
> It may be, is emerging or has just
> Collapsed.

Stevens's canto is a variation on Nietzsche's image of Greek theatre. The edifice of the theatre is engulfed by the clouds; it becomes a cloud. If the house is the habitation of a family, then the theatre, at least in Nietzsche's terms, is the habitation of the community. It is the space in which the community represents to itself the titanic powers of nature and its relation to them. And here Stevens shows how even this representational space is engulfed by that which it would represent.

It is at this point that the scholar, one of the community's 'major men' walks out into the midst of the auroral changes. In their context of the poem and Stevens's life work, the lines that I quoted at the start of this reading take on the resonance of Dickinson's plank in reason breaking. A whole world is nudged off its axis and the human mind is left reeling, in Stevens's case, reeling through the natural changes of the auroras. With less risk and more poise, Stevens at the beginning of his career in 'To the One of the Fictive Music' (CP 87) remarked:

> Now, of the music summoned by the birth
> That separates us from the wind and sea,
> Yet leaves us in them, until earth becomes,
> By being so much of the things we are,
> Gross effigy and simulacrum [. . .]

It is as if Stevens throws Jameson's accusation back at him: to pay attention only to the gross effigies and simulacrums of social and cultural semantics laundered of their origin in nature and landscape is to avoid 'reality'; it is to avoid the hermeneutic complexities that the natural world presents to an observer whose intelligence is not limited, like the rationalists of 'Six Significant Landscapes', by the hats on their heads and the rooms they are sitting in, that is, by these man-made enclosures, these sheltering fictions. The imagination that is truly capable will take the risk of walking out of the house in flames, of moving beyond the gross effigies and simulacrums that humanity weaves about itself and into nature. Perhaps a post-modern rejoinder to this would be that there is no end run to 'reality', there is no escape from simulacrum, and that Stevens's nostalgia for the *Ding-an-sich* is hopelessly nostalgic and naïve. But to respond thus is to fail to perceive the subtlety of the poems. The 'reality' that Stevens finds in landscape and nature is not some solid basis on which psychologies and polities may be safely built, but rather the place where all such systems are recognised *as* simulacra and fictions.

In Canto IX, terrible visions of physical and metaphysical exposure to the elements present themselves in the wake of the scholar's walking out to face the sky in flames. The image of nakedness here is not yet positive since all our previous fictions that sheltered us from the elements have been discarded and we are at our most vulnerable. And yet this can also be the point of inflexion, where humanity having faced the elements is able to begin again from that 'savage source' and renegotiate its position in the world. That is what happens in the last canto when the rabbi chants the phases of the differences between the people and the world. He meditates a whole (cf., the 'holiness' of VIII; and more generally, Stevens love of the word's cognates, 'hale' and 'health'). We are in a church of sorts: 'congregation' evokes both the Israelites in the wilderness, and also the Congregationalists in the American wilderness (for an excellent discussion of the biblical background to the poem, see Cook 128–33). The house with the mother's tender presence is debased, dilapidated into the 'hall harridan', a habitation that tallies with the unhappiness of humanity. This is the structure that suffices.

Thus we are left with an image of an unidealised human habitation in the midst of the elements. One of the frequent accusations levelled against certain American writers is that in order to write their great odes of the individual imagination, incandescent with Adamic freshness, they had to erase public contexts, and occasionally racial injustice, on a massive scale (see Morrison and also Rowe). James Longenbach argues that Stevens in the phase of his career after writing 'Notes Toward a Supreme Fiction' to the end of *The Auroras of Autumn* loses touch with 'the plain sense of things' that informed the best of his earlier poetry and would return again in *The Rock*. The catastrophes and crises conjured in 'The Auroras', for instance, are resolved too easily. He is surely correct when he says that the poem is 'less involved with the crises of its time' (289). He also remarks how 'although a poem like "An Ordinary Evening in New Haven" appears to have a more "open" form than the symmetrically designed "Notes Toward a Supreme Fiction," that apparent openness is sustained only because "An Ordinary Evening" rehearses the achieved vision of "Notes"' (290); this is true of 'The Auroras' also.

I see this differently. Poems like 'The Auroras' and 'An Ordinary Evening in New Haven' are the crowning achievements of the vision he was moving towards in earlier work like the 'Notes'. The *maestoso* rhetoric of 'The Auroras' builds toward the crisis mid-way through in Canto VI and then spreads outwards in the remaining cantos, comprehending everything from the cosmos to the community huddled at the end in 'hall harridan'. In its structuring it is a much less experimental poem than the 'Notes', which engages us with its unexpected jumps of focus and tone from one canto to the next. 'The Auroras', in comparison, seems more fated in its trajectory: there are no Arabs jumping through the window in the moonlight, no Chaplin figures at the edge of the town, no mock-serious dismissals of wrens; instead there is a prophetic intoning, a confrontation of the *Moira* in the manner of the great Greek tragedies (and indeed Melpomene figures in one of the short poems in the collection). However, what is most important in both poems is that they move towards a communal vision. The heroic imagination that does this is the imagination of the community, not some Emersonian transparent eyeball. For instance, the scholar who undergoes the crisis in Canto VI does not narrate the poem, but is just one more episode in the movement toward the congregation gathered beneath the sky at the end of the poem, singing the phases of difference. And even the rabbi there is not really comparable to the Adamic Emersonian visionary; his role is more pastoral, more practical, while also being the custodian of matters of the spirit.

Ghosting the poem is Stevens's awareness of the history of the community in its region (i.e., the 'ancestral course' of Canto II): for Stevens himself, the region of his father and mother and the habitations that he would return to seventy years later was Reading, Pennsylvania, and as the amount of books that he possessed on the area's history attests, he was keenly aware of the 'ancestral course' there and his own imagination as part of a larger community. I shall discuss some of those attachments in Chapter Five, but for now I wish to emphasise the way the poem explores the phases of the difference between the community and the land it inhabits; this places it in the central line of Stevens's thought throughout his career on the relations between nature, politics and social contexts in general. But, the response might come, what use are such explorations if they do not give on to contemporaneous crises in the way that, say, 'The Man with the Blue Guitar' does? One response to this is: what use is the 'The Man with the Blue Guitar' to us if it gives on to debates we no longer care about? Such questions concern not just Stevens but the value of historicist criticism and of literature in general. Only scholars read poems to see how they connect with contemporaneous political and social contexts. It is an exercise than can often be of interest, but its implication is that an artwork's engagement with contemporaneous political events is the most important aesthetic criterion; and such an implication is a treason of the clerks. My argument might seem a throwback to the time of the New Critics, universalism, etc., but what I am arguing for is a special mode in poetry, the kind we find in 'The Auroras', that provides readers with visions of themselves and their communities against huge horizons, here of nature; without these expansive visions of, if you like, political archetypes, a poetry that engages the political in more detailed ways is meaningless. In order to think politically a community has to have images of itself; and that this mode does not directly address contemporaneous crises does not mean that it reneges on its responsibilities to the community. A language of ceremony is necessary that does not shut out the political and social but that enables us to think more acutely and widely about social formations.

In the present critical climate, such claims are suspect since they are made by many who wish to exclude political considerations from the appreciation of literature, in order to keep it a precinct of pure spirit and private emotion. But that too is wrong. A poetry of transcendence and the spirit is necessary that can foster emotional allegiances not just within the sphere of the personal but to formations of the community also. Unlike most poems that seek to make such connections, 'The Auroras of Autumn' moves from the private (the mother, the father) into the collective. Charles Altieri, in a lecture on Whitman and the nation, remarks how Whitman makes a similar move in order 'to capture what seems most intimate in our attachments to the world, then extend that intimacy so that is carried as passion into the public sphere by the poet's eloquence' ('Spectacular Anti-Spectacle'). Altieri goes on to illustrate this point not with readings of, say, the jingoistic poems at the beginning of *Drum-Taps* but of 'Crossing Brooklyn Ferry', one of Whitman's great poems of interiority, but also a poem that also spreads out to comprehend and blood the nation with thought, showing the way that the spots of time of the individual imagination can take on public valency and also forge the allegiances of other individuals to larger units.

Altieri's argument here is related to a wider dissatisfaction with the climate of criticism in the US at the moment:

> Whitman wants a writing that can fully inhabit the emotional registers evoked when we reflect on our relations to the nation, that is to the social construction with the power to produce meanings for our actions so compelling that they can lead us to sacrifice our immediate interests and even our lives. Conversely, our contemporary cult of differences is so committed to unsettling these social structures that it reserves for itself precious little common ground on which to base large scale social projects redressing the evils that it exposes. Whitman's version of the social requires that poetry be able to so link wording and willing that the work's articulateness generates, sustains, and justifies the most intense and capacious affirmations that agents can perform. ('Spectacular Anti-Spectacle')

Although Stevens's attitude to nation was very different from Whitman's, . Altieri's comment is a good description of the movement of 'The Auroras' and suggests why the ceremonious rhetoric of the poem is so important to it. To acknowledge 'The Auroras' as public poetry is to recognise the need for imaginative formations in polities that can command emotional allegiance. The moment of transcendence here is that of the collective, not of some Werther on a hilltop. And it is worth noting that Stevens's community at the end of the poem is provisional, open, aware of its element. It is a public vision that is in stark contrast to the reactionary retrenchments of the 1950s in the US, and it is one that is still of value in the US today for its creation of the kind of 'common ground' that Charles Altieri discusses above. This is what Stevens seeks out in the poem, and its location is landscape and nature, the human gathering huddled beneath the magnificent changes arching and swerving through the sky, 'to a haggling of wind and weather', in the midst of '[t]hese fields, these hills, these tinted distances, / And the pines above and along and beside the sea'. Leaving our enclosures for a vision of this, we rediscover social formation and learn to think in ways that seek to fulfil not just individual satisfactions but those of the community also.

Chapter 4

The city, the landscape, the masses

1

In 'Imagination as Value', Stevens says that 'we live today in a time dominated by great masses of men' (NA 142); this is a fact of modern reality that Stevens tries to confront in his poetry of the 1930s and early 1940s. He does not take up a particular political stance to do this: as he repeatedly points out in *The Necessary Angel* that is not the job of the poet at all. Rather the poet must comprehend modern reality if his work is to fulfil Stevens's stated aim for poetry, that is to help people live their lives. In this chapter I argue that as he confronts his 'time dominated by great masses of men', Stevens's greatest fund is the horizon of nature. In order to comprehend the significance of those masses and his age, he constantly turned to landscape and nature as calibration and confirmation, as a way of testing the reality of all conceptions of the masses of men. In Chapter One I discussed the way that Stevens tries to connect the exaltations of the individual imagination abroad in nature with public contexts and social forms. Here we have another variation on this as Stevens figures forth images of humanity by the million and tries to take its measure by relating it to the natural world.

Stated this way it sounds slightly strange: how can you 'take humanity's measure' by comparing it with landscape? What could possibly result from such a comparison? Of course it would be wrong to expect from poetry the same kind of result as we would from a sociological or geographical comparison, but nevertheless it does seem worth inquiring on a basic level what motivates Stevens to make such a comparison. My answer is that for Stevens nature is where the human imagination experiences its most intense feelings of vision and exaltation, and as such is a kind of benchmark against which all human configurations must be measured. In his journals from his time in New York as young man he carefully records those moments of intense feeling in the midst of the countryside. I have already quoted Frank Lentricchia when he says that 'Stevens's terms are antitranscendental and naturalistic, atheistic and aestheticist; but with Emerson he tends to believe that these moments of vitality cannot happen in the streets of our cities' (*Modernist Quartet* 137). Nevertheless, Stevens having experienced those moments of vitality presses on to discover how they relate to the streets of his cities, that is, how the visions seen in nature can be related to social configurations. The city or town, with its dense population, it clusters of buildings, its concentration of thoroughfares, its intense commercial activity, is perhaps the strongest image of social formation in general: when one thinks of millions of men, or the great masses, the image of the city immediately comes to mind. Later in this chapter I shall trace this journey in reverse as Stevens begins in the middle of a town, New Haven, and works his way outwards as the poem progresses into the surrounding land- and seascapes in order to find out how the mind's exaltations in nature relate to the city; or, in other words, how can we live in cities while still maintaining our apprehension of those exaltations.

Stevens, in general, unlike his friend Carl Sandburg, or other contemporaneous poets like Hart Crane or Edgar Lee Masters, is not a poet of the city. (Even when he writes of New Haven he has to leave it in the end for the open spaces of its environs.) He does not feel that in order to confront modernity one must confront the potent sign of the modern. Of course, he does have some poems of the city, but he is decidedly uneasy in the urban environment. He writes of 'loneliness in Jersey City' or the bleak urban vista of 'The Common Life'. Exaltation and jubilation are things that might be experienced by witnessing the metamorphoses of the weather above the city, but that is something else altogether. He does, however, occasionally toss the great masses of humanity up into that very weather and study their trajectory through the air in order to get at their meaning. He also frequently compares those masses with an object taken out of nature, for instance, a flower. Another favourite move, especially in *Transport to Summer* and *The Auroras of Autumn*, is to take on the voice of the community as it considers a landscape or a natural object. In many poems the moment of exaltation in nature is related to social forms through Stevens's location of a town nearby, thus letting us know that the extremes of consciousness experienced in nature must eventually be transmitted to the adjacent community. 'The Idea of Order at Key West', is, for instance, about the attempt to relate a community of listeners in the midst of natural beauty. Working out those communal meanings is the body of the poem.

In the pages that follow I shall look at some examples of this pattern, which is, I believe, fundamental to Stevens's art. This is his way of facing modern reality, of finding images that will suffice and help us to think about the ways we live our lives, the way we think about social configurations and the images we have for them. We can't call such thinking political in the usual sense of the word; nevertheless, politics deals in images we have of ourselves collectively and insofar as Stevens does just this in his poetry his imagination is reaching into the realms of social form. He is writing the poem of the earth, aware that the earth is the place of foliage, blossoms, expansive natural scenery, but it is also where the great masses of men disport themselves, changing from one political configuration to another, from one generation to the next. His sense was that these activities take place within the same space and that the phases of their relations must be explored.

The first important poem in which Stevens sings those phases is 'The Man with the Blue Guitar' (CP 165–84). That the poem is about communal meanings is evident from the start:

> The man bent over his blue guitar,
> A shearsman of sorts. The day was green.
>
> They said, 'You have a blue guitar,
> You do not play things as they are.'

Here we have the figure of the artist confronted by something like a chorus in Greek tragedy, whose task was to mediate the public significance of the events on the stage. The task of the guitarist here though is not just to sing about the green day, but also to find images for the great masses of people; his song must be one that carries, as Canto IV has it, 'A million people on one string', while not losing sight of the intricacies of individual feeling that 'crazily, craftily call'. Over a decade before 'Imagination as Value', Stevens formulated the need for art to comprehend modern reality and face the great masses of men that characterise it. This cannot be resolved or answered purely in the sphere of the urban, that is, the sign of the modern; Stevens, in a gesture that would be come very frequent in his later poetry, ranges out toward the calibrating presences of the sun and moon, land and sea, summer fields and mountain forests. If the images and melody to accommodate a million people on one string are to be found then it is the panorama of nature that must be invoked:

> It is the sun that shares our works.
> The moon shares nothing. It is a sea.
>
> When shall I come to say of the sun,
> It is a sea; it shares nothing;
>
> The sun no longer shares our work
> And the earth is alive with creeping men,
>
> Mechanical beetles never quite warm?   (VII)

Then in the next canto a 'vivid, florid, turgid sky' is figured and the relation sought between it and the twang of the guitar. Canto IX also has the guitarist going further into the weather, and not until X does Stevens remind us that the main requirement of the song is that it accommodate a 'million people on one string', that it face modern reality with its great masses of men. In his commonplace book, Stevens noted Jacques Maritain's statement that 'the artist has a chance of reshaping the whole mass' (Stevens, *Sur Plusieurs* 59). In Canto X there is a scene of celebration in the city for the demagogue ('Harry Truman as god' [L 789]), but this figure and the social formations he creates give nothing of the sun or the moon, and the following canto topples his regime as the repressed (the land and sea) returns to overwhelm the society of the demagogue:

> Women become

> The cities, children become the fields
> And men in waves become the sea.

> It is the chord that falsifies.
> The sea returns upon the men,

> The field entrap the children [. . .]

And so the variations continue through the poem, modulating back and forth between the natural world and the need to comprehend the masses. This is an attempt to relate the 'generation's dream', as the final canto has it, with the elements of the landscape, 'The imagined pine, the imagined jay'. In his excellent extended reading of the poem, Alan Filreis demonstrates how '[i]n reproducing an ideologically contentious environment in its very structure, the poem itself organized the disarray of literary-political conditions that would come to judge it' (*Modernism* 279). He carefully follows the path the poem's complex dialogic movement as it threads a way through the political and cultural debates of the 1930s. Reading the conclusion of the poem, he says that this is not a reversion to some kind of lyrical space untouched by the space of politics, but rather that the poet must acknowledge both the imagination and social forms: 'The end of the poem makes thematically clear what the interactive structure of the whole implies all along – that modern poetry overtly and incessantly lyric is no different from other forms of political language in inscribing opposing voices; that each discourse entails a response to other discourses' (*Modernism* 279). So much of poetry criticism either denies political contexts or worse still (and what is more frequent) crudely imposes an ideological critique. Filreis is correct here in saying that poetry, in Stevens's view, should respond to other discourses (political, cultural, economic), but that does not mean that the discourse of poetry is no different from these in other respects. Rather, poetry's advantage when making such a response lies in the fact that it is in most respects very different. That difference is most obvious exactly when we consider Stevens's use of nature in the poem. Rather than attacking political and cultural debate head on, the natural imagery that is everywhere in 'The Man With the Blue Guitar' allows him a crucial distance as he navigates through the warring opinions. This, together with Stevens's belief that nature is the site of the spirit's intensest rendezvous, the place where access to 'reality' is acutest, makes for a special type of pastoral. There is space for the imagination's mercies, but playing through them also are the urgencies and voices of conflicting ideologies.

The brief poem, 'Memorandum' (op 116), a decade later, more strenuously demands the calibration of political configurations by objects out of nature and confronts the human masses. With its confrontation of those masses it is not typical of Stevens's later work, which is as I shall show in general more concerned with community. There is none of the dialogic variations of 'The Man with the Blue Guitar', but the frame of reference is the same:

> Say this to Pravda, tell the damned rag
> That the peaches are slowly ripening.
>
> . . . .
>
> Millions hold millions in their arms.

This is not Stevens rejecting the grimy world of politics for the eternities of nature. It is a cry of frustration, of the same stock that we saw in 'Esthétique du Mal' in Chapter Two, against certain types of politics that suppress parts of the world in order to make their interpretations fit. A good politics, that is, not the simplistic paradigms of Marxism, must be able to comprehend a plenitude of phenomena, from the natural world to the amours of millions of citizens. What is interesting here though is Stevens's choice to avoid the more sentimental image of a single pair of lovers at the poem's end in favour of the gaze of a kind of amatory census-taker, who surveys the whole United States and sees part of the population joined in loving conjunction.

But this relation between the masses and nature is not always so positive. As the Secretary for Porcelain observes in Section II of 'Extracts from Addresses to the Academy of Fine Ideas' (cp 252–9), it can be perverted. One of Martin Heidegger's very few references to the Holocaust after the war concerned the dangers of considering people as masses: their extermination then takes on the same character as an agricultural experiment or a tourist industry that processes groups of people through scenic places (quoted in Safranski 414). Stevens's point is the same: if ten thousand deaths can be equated with an emperor's apricot or eggplant then something is very wrong. The *Weltanschauung* invented by the maker of catastrophe is one in which the whim of a ruler for a piece of fruit carries the same valency as his genocidal ambitions; and this is evil to the core. There must be a way to think through the expanses of politics with its masses of men in a more humane way than this. Stevens's modus operandi is to take a side step: rather than a wringing of hands he heads out into open country. Thus, in Section IV, a poet figure absconds from the academy to the surrounding winter hills and tries to confront reality there. The passage is remarkable for its is direct simple narrative after two pages of clotted imagery and argument:

On an early Sunday morning in April, a feeble day,
He felt curious about the winter hills
And wondered about the water in the lake.
It had been cold since December. Snow fell, first,
At New Year and, from then until April, lay
On everything. Now it had melted, leaving
The gray grass like a pallet, closely pressed;
And dirt. The wind blew in the empty place.
The winter wind blew in an empty place –
There was that difference between the and an,
The difference between himself and no man,
No man that heard a wind in an empty place.

. . . .

                                                    If,
When he looked, the water ran up the air or grew white
Against the edge of the ice, the abstraction would
Be broken and winter would be broken and done,
And being would be being himself again,
Being, becoming seeing and feeling and self,
Black water breaking into reality.

The observation of the landscape is minute and the speaker, through the conditional tense, conveys the importance of the rhythms of nature to the rhythms of thought. We have moved a long way from the tone of the first two sections. Here an individual escapes the eye invented by the maker of catastrophe and experiences access to reality in the midst of the landscape. The participles in the penultimate line above convey the invigoration and excitement of returning to the natural world. This, however, is not an escapist move, since this excursion serves a very clear purpose for the academy and the community in general. It clears the field of vision of all irrelevancies and brings the relations between people considered as masses of humanity and the world into focus, and rights the distortions of the maker of catastrophe of Section II. This is the value of '[e]cstatic identities / Between oneself and the weather and the things / Of the weather' (VII): they renovate our apprehension of the social formations that political power organises us into. Nothing is greater witness of this than the voicing of the final section, where the detached theoretical tone of the Secretary for Porcelain is abandoned for the moral strength and lucid tone of: 'We live in a camp . . .'. Now the speaker admits his own membership of the great masses of humanity, that he too is implicated and cannot escape the world through scholarly contemplation of it. Also worth remarking is how the academy has been transformed into a camp, a much coarser habitation, and one that allows no respite from the awareness of the martial aspects of life at that time.

We find this dependency between landscape and the great masses of humanity also in 'Repetitions of a Young Captain' (CP 306–10) in *Transport to Summer*. Once again Stevens, by turning to the natural world, is able to make sense of the panorama of millions of men that he is presented with. At the poem's beginning a previous mode of representation, the theatre, has been destroyed by new political and martial transformations: 'A tempest cracked on the theatre. Quickly, / The wind beat in the roof and half the walls.' In Section III we discover that this is no ordinary tempest: 'Millions of major men against their like / Make more than thunder's rural rumbling'. A new mode of representation, a new figural system, must be discovered so that we can think about this new order. It is nature that provides this in Section V. The repeated word in this section, 'memorandum', is possibly picked up by Stevens in the later poem of that title, which I discussed earlier and which deals with the same subject. Similarly the section ends with the same turn of thought: the private concerns of the individual (in 'Memorandum', of two lovers) are placed in the context of the great masses of men. Just as Paul Valéry in *La Jeune Parque* (1917) was able to make sense of the ravages of World War I by imagining the voice of a Fate as she observes the panoramas of mountains and seas, so too Stevens here turns to those expanses in order to find the significance of those thunderous millions of men introduced in Section III. This is the moment of revelation, as in Section IV of 'Extracts', which renovates social formations and public discourse. The turn rejects gigantic formations that cannot comprehend private emotion, but that does not entail a rejection of public discourse in toto. There is another way, which refuses the expanses that the armies set for themselves (as opposed to only the expanses of nature) in favour of an oratory that is instinct with the verdurous tropisms of nature:

> Green is the orator
> Of our passionate height. He wears a tufted green,
> And tosses green for those for whom green speaks.
>
> Secrete us in reality. It is there
> My orator. Let this giantness fall down
> And come to nothing. Let the rainy arcs
>
> And pathetic magnificences dry in the sky.
> Secrete us in reality. Discover
> A civil nakedness in which to be,
>
> In which to bear with the exactest force
> The precisions of fate, nothing fobbed off, nor changed
> In a beau language without a drop of blood.

This is Stevens at his most affirmative, indeed solemn, where his poetry comes near the seriousness of religious ceremony. But even at such a juncture the language must be 'beau' – the French usage a dandyish flourish in the liturgy of the priest.

This interview between the great masses of men and landscape, between society and nature, is figured in another way in Stevens's poetry. Joseph Brodsky once remarked that there are certain locales that continually draw poets back because they have a certain atmosphere, a slant of light or architectural arrangement, which enables their imaginations to extend themselves; his was a sea port with neoclassical porticoes that had seen better days – somewhat like his native St Petersburg. In Stevens's poetry we find there is a certain mise-en-scène, a particular arrangement of the landscape that is especially germane to him and elicits some of his most intense imaginative moments when he thinks about the relations between human communities and the world in which they live. It embodies the elements that I have been discussing so far in 'The Man with the Blue Guitar', 'Memorandum' and 'Repetitions of a Young Captain', but whereas in these poems, especially the first and last, the arrangement of community and nature was, to say the least, jaunty and provisional (viz., the millions hanging in mid-earth at the end of Section V of 'Repetitions'), Stevens often chooses an arrangement that is in all respects more down to earth. For him this is a precinct that includes magisterial elements of natural scenery (mountains, rivers, the sea) but also human dwellings, often gathered into communities. The poem moves between these two poles, just as in 'How to Live. What to Do' the speaker faced the transcendent vision on the mountaintop, all the time aware that he must relate what he experienced there to a public context. For instance, in 'Mrs Alfred Uruguay' (CP 248–50), there is the farcical scramble for transcendence played out on the mountain, but nearby there are the villages that the figure of capable imagination goes down to at the poem's end, energising the dreams of the citizens there ('The villages slept as the capable man went down, / Time swished on the village clocks and dreams were alive'). The physical geography of Reading and its environs, with mountains adjacent to the town, obviously left its mark on the larger forms of Stevens's thought. The configuration is often that of the sky contrasted with the town or houses lying below it. The supreme poem in this mode is 'The Auroras of Autumn', which although it begins with a solitary figure, ends with the image of the rabbi gathering the community in 'hall harridan' beneath the magisterial metamorphoses sweeping through the skies.

Other poems that come to mind are Section II of 'Esthétique du Mal (CP 314–15), 'Evening without Angels' (CP 136–8), 'Of Hartford in a Purple Light' (226–7); in 'Contrary Theses (II)' (CP 270) the city with it different activities is juxtaposed with 'the grand mechanics of earth and sky'; in 'A Woman Sings for a Soldier Come Home' (CP 360–1) the speaker remarks how 'The clouds are over the village, the town, / To which the walker speaks / And tells his wound', ending 'Just out of the village, at its edge, / In the quiet there'; 'Forces, the Will & the

Weather' (CP 228–9) puts the community in the balance against the huge tensions going on in the sky as the seasons change. Critics like Alan Filreis who are so alive to the contemporaneous social contexts of Stevens's poetry find these moments somewhat escapist:

> The contrary theses, for instance, of 'Contrary Theses (II)' (1942) are the abstract, 'grand mechanics' of nature on the one hand, and observed social particularities, 'The negroes playing football in the park,' on the other (CP 270). The 'contrary' was negotiable insofar as 'The flies / And the bees *still* sought the chrysanthemums' odor' [Filreis's italics] (CP 270), no matter how dire the economic or how tense the political circumstance. (*Modernism* 237)

And, commenting on one of Stevens's projected poems, he surmises how 'the confusions and intrusions of the social world would routinely terminate in the natural, even in the "picnic sense" of the metropolitan park' (237). Leaving aside the fact that there is no dire social circumstance registered in 'Contrary Theses (II)', I want to dispute his dismissal here of the natural. When we look at Stevens's treatment of nature across the wider span of his career, we see that he does not use it as some merely routine resolution or escape hatch. Even in 'The Man with the Blue Guitar', a poem that Filreis praises for its exemplary treatment of conflicting ideological standpoints, the horizons of nature play a central role, as I showed above.

As we move through *Transport to Summer* to *The Auroras of Autumn*, this kind of poem that tries to fit a million people on one string begins to disappear and is replaced by a different type that has, instead of an image of a town or village adjacent to the landscape, the collective voice of the community addressing nature or objects taken from it. This is part of a larger shift in the voicing of Stevens's poetry in his later years as he more frequently opts for the first-person plural; this in turn reflects his deepening interest in what communities make of themselves and the world they live in. Connected with this is Stevens's interest in his own genealogy and we increasingly see references to the course of generations, instead of the earlier lone figures of *Harmonium*. For instance, we are given no idea of the family past of the woman in 'Sunday Morning', or even of Crispin, and while in his later work he does not sketch out particular family histories, he is intensely interested in the formal mechanisms of the transmission of cultural and ethical values from one generation to the next. Place is important in this transmission, as one of Stevens's ideas that didn't change from the time of 'Anecdote of Men by the Thousand' to the end was that 'There are men of a province / Who are that province' (CP 51); this kind of osmosis can only happen over many generations.

Negotiations with the landscape are carried out by the speakers of 'Study of Images I' (CP 463–4) from *The Auroras of Autumn*. The sentence 'It is, we are' almost begs, mid-way through, a Cartesian 'ergo', and makes clear the dependency of community on its place, its surrounding landscape. 'Continual Conversation with a Silent Man' (CP 359–60) from the previous collection is voiced by a community also and negotiates its relation with the landscape: 'The old brown hen and the old blue sky, / Between the two we live and die'. One of the 'never-ending things' that is referred to later is the way 'the many meanings in the leaves // [are] Brought down to one below the eaves'.

The late poem, 'Americana' (OP 121), brings together crowds and landscape and, in a more overt way than Section IV of 'Credences', confronts the historical aspect of the land of America. Whereas for earlier writers like Emerson and Whitman that land was unstoried, Stevens registers the fact that many generations have lived on it and changed its aspect and changed also the way people live in it. At the same time he also registers the need for the verve and vision of the Adamic moment that so entranced Whitman, and, at least earlier in his career, Emerson. Also, as in the earlier poems I discussed, there is a confrontation between the great masses of men, with their modes of thought that serve to obscure rather than illuminate the place they live, and the natural world. It is not a poem that I would want to make any large claims for: as is occasionally the case with Stevens's late uncollected poems, what is expressed with nuance and power elsewhere, is too programmatic and simplistic. In phrases like 'in a health of the weather' and 'the deadly general of men' one feels that Stevens is on auto-pilot; even a line like 'Flaunts that first fortune, which he wanted so much' only serves to remind of the better poems in which Stevens used similar phrasing (i.e., 'Large Red Man Reading': 'And spoke the feeling for them, which was what they had lacked' [CP 424]). But in the connections that it makes between the landscape and the generations of a community that have lived in it, it is of interest. If society loses that feeling of first fortune then it stagnates. The move is similar to that of 'Repetitions of a Young Captain': the need for the 'green orator' is the same as that for the feelings of the 'first soothsayers of the land'. But where 'Repetitions' is concerned with the dislocations of reality brought about by way of war, here Stevens, in the small scope of this lyric, encompasses the sweep of US history from colony to present day, figuring it as a trajectory that moves away from the land and away from ideas of community toward the great masses of men.

I wish to turn now to another poem that depicts a bleak moment for the American imagination – 'The Common Life' (CP 221). Here there is no playfulness concerning the idea of man's accord with the land, no ironic supposition that the land is a woman and no immigrant to transform the landscape with a new vocabulary. Stevens looks squarely at the modern American industrial town and produces a poem with a factual tone, employing short sentences and none of his usual syntactical legerdemain. As Alan Filreis says, the poem is 'not an expression of contempt for this commonality so much as knowing commiseration' (277). There are no recondite elliptical metaphors demanding lengthy elucidation. Perhaps it is the mention of the electric plant, a phrase that strikes one as strange in a poem by Stevens, in the first stanza, that secures this tone for the rest of the poem. Two forms of energy – spiritual and technological – are represented by reference to their architectural embodiment. If you like, they are two aspects of the American dream. Steeples hold bells but also signify, from Gothic times, a yearning toward God, toward spiritual perfection. Electricity makes other promises. It runs the forces of manufacturing, its tiny impulses trickle through transistors, electronic circuits, the screens that present the texts one reads and adjusts. Its promise is that technology will make the world a better place. The poem catches both these movements in the middle of their significations of promise, and 'friezes' ('That's the downtown frieze') them in order to examine what they are in relation to the place they are and the space they have produced, instead of in the context of what they say they *shall* provide. In the way that it calls a halt to these two institutions, and examines the immediate perception of them instead of what they promise, it is quite an unburgherly poem. After all, the institutions of technology and religion are two aspects of what we can loosely call the bourgeois project for both spiritual and worldly happiness and security.

Whatever Left Stevens meant he was moving towards when he discussed Stanley Burnshaw's review of his work, in this poem we can get an idea of some of Stevens's dissatisfactions with the United States of his time (L 286). He would never have held, as some Marxist critics would, that in such an American industrial town as depicted in 'The Common Life', it is the productive labour of the workers that is hidden by the spatial practice that produced such 'flat air'. Stevens disdained the lionisation of the working man that was taking hold in the American intellectual circles of his time (see Longenbach 135–47, and L 286). But something was being hidden, something was lost:

> It is a morbid light
> In which they stand,
> Like an electric lamp
> On a page of Euclid.

The poem says that here in this American industrial town, with this institutional spatial practice, men are dehumanised and women are no longer desirable to men. On a deeper level, these sentiments connect with a theme that would become more important to Stevens over the following years: marriage. In 'Notes Toward a Supreme Fiction', he circles this idea in different ways, and he suggests, albeit in an ironic tone, that marriage is much more than just a relationship between a man and a woman – it also has to do with the land they live in, the place they are (CP 401). In 'The Common Life', because of the 'morbid light' (*morbus*, diseased) that shines on the town, men and women cannot couple, cannot marry. This sounds somewhat ridiculous until you widen the connotative scope of the term 'marriage': marriage is an event when opposites meet and form something radically new, when the immigrant marries the indigene and they enrich and renovate all around them.

The echoes of Greece through the poem subtly remind the reader of the decay of a once great civilisation. The point made is that this Euclidean light that turns land into a geometer's sheet, is a disease, a wrong. This poem 'friezes' in its gaze the effects of such thinking and practice and judges them for the morbidity they have created through their interpretation and transformation of the land.

2

The moment of Romantic exaltation in the midst of nature in writers like Emerson and Wordsworth was bought, as I have remarked already, at the expense of engagement with society. The individual imagination absconds from the ties of friendship, family and responsibility to float freely through the land-scape, experiencing a visionary expansion of consciousness. Stevens valued this moment, but the axis upon which so many of his poems turn connects such transcendent matters of nature with social forms. Romantic poets in general avoided cities when searching out moments of transcendence; for Stevens one of the greatest challenges of his career was to write a long poem about the city without losing sight of such moments. As he stated when writing 'An Ordinary Evening in New Haven' (CP 465–89): 'my interest is to try to get as close to the ordinary, the commonplace and the ugly as it is possible for a poet to get' (L 636), terms that Stevens would never have applied to the natural world, but that, after my reading of 'The Common Life', look like a good description of the city as subject matter. In this poem he wanted to confront urban reality as directly as possible in order, as he went on to comment in the letter to Bernard Heringman, 'to purge oneself of anything false'. The city, as well as being a set of physical objects, is also a kind of communal congeries, of individuals dreaming them-selves to be different things. The glue that keeps a city together is the fact that its people imagine collectively – imagine a set of laws to live by and fantasies to yearn towards. In this poem, Stevens is especially sensitive to the collective nature of myth-making, of the ways in which a community must imagine its heavens and hells, high ceremonies and exalted beliefs. But the turn I detect in 'An Ordinary Evening in New Haven', and that I shall show in the reading that follows, is towards nature as horizon for this kind of communal dreaming.

The poem has, at times, the élan of humorous improvisation while, at others, it achieves convincing rhetorical solemnity that is rare in twentieth-century poetry. Perhaps because of its length and difficulty it does not enjoy the same popularity of, say, a poem like 'Sunday Morning'; Stevens himself admitted that it might 'seem diffuse and casual' (L 719). And yet it brings together the central preoccupations of Stevens's poetic career. That makes it all the more difficult to comprehend why it has been more or less ignored by recent critics of Stevens. Its rhetorical modes are various, ranging from the anecdotal to the hierophantic. Having no narrative unity other than that of the poet walking around New

Haven, what holds the poem together is the way in which Stevens negotiates the turns from one canto to the next. It is in these *volte* that we see the strength of Stevens's imagination at so late a stage in his life.

The substantiality, or onticality, of the houses and buildings in New Haven is put in question, and one of the main inquiries of the poems is: of what are these houses composed? Physical things, yes, but they also have significance as the type of representative space. The idea of the nation is also pertinent as Stevens refers to the origin of the town as a colony. Indeed, the poem is interesting for the way that it recuperates the freshness of vision, the flauntings of first fortune, that the colonisers of the land must have experienced. This vision is one that provides a vision of the 'brilliancy at the central of the earth'. As it ends, the poem turns to the space of the surrounding landscape of Connecticut, in this way providing an answer to its opening question as to the composition of the houses. The habitations cannot be solely composed of ourselves, the poem concludes, but must be *of* the landscape and nature of the place. They are makings of the sun and sea and fields and mountains of that place. By apprehending this, Stevens, in the final canto, is able to apprehend the most fleeting but transcendent moments of vision in the midst of 'the ordinary, the commonplace and the ugly' of the city.

This 'central' is not some solid hypostasis, a fixed tableau, to be appropriated by the community of the town, and subordinated to it. Rather, as Bonnie Costello says of Stevens's landscapes in general it is 'pragmatic and provisional, affording aesthetic and emotional if not intellectual arrival' ('Adequacy' 204). It is the horizon to which he must turn to make sense of social forms and urban configurations. As I showed in Chapter Three, this interview between nature and human fictions – be they houses, paintings, or cities – is an interview between a plenitude of interpretive possibilities the enclosures of humanity. This former is the zone into which he moves as the poem reaches its conclusion.

These considerations evolve from the long tradition of thought on the Romantic sublime as a revelatory moment in which a man becomes aware of an agency beyond his control, and yet one with which he (as we are talking of a male poet) may align himself as he writes the poem of this moment. The dynamic of the sublime interview is still relevant here since what is disclosed in nature is a space that exists prior to man and all his fictional spaces. What Stevens's poem seeks is to know what the town is, what any space is which mankind constructs, and finds that he can only begin to answer the question if these spaces are construed as *within* nature. What the poem ultimately insists on is that although the community's habitations, their 'fictional spaces', their collective dreamings, give on to that of nature, they are limited and contained within this prior space that has not been controlled and shaped by its agency, but that cannot be apprehended as some solid basis. Stevens sends us into zones that are uncertain but that are also full of rich possibilities for the imagination.

What is striking about the first canto is the title above it. It immediately situates the whole meditation in the town of New Haven itself. It is noteworthy that Stevens did not choose a larger city: he knew New York well, but maybe agreed with William Carlos Williams when he said that it was 'too big, too much a congeries of the entire world's facets' (Williams xiii). (Of course, what was also important is that Stevens worked on it through the summer of 1949 and read a shortened version at a meeting of the Connecticut Academy of Arts and Sciences in November.) New Haven, like Paterson, offered something graspable, something the poet's imagination could work around instead of getting lost in, as arguably Hart Crane did in *The Bridge*. As the houses and buildings of New Haven change in the failing light, part of their substance must also appear to fail, or at least to retire for the night, so that the poet is prompted to ask: 'Of what is this house composed if not of the sun, // These houses, these difficult objects [?]'. Canto II proposes an answer: 'Suppose these houses are composed of ourselves'. At the end of Canto I, the poem and the town come together to form a 'festival sphere', a rotund mythological figure, but this resolution is too premature and is curtly dismissed by the supposition that opens Canto II. Here Stevens proposes 'ourselves', the society of the town, as its creators, and the town is maintained, it seems, by this community's perpetual imagining of itself. The rest of the poem generates itself from the poet's dissatisfaction with this preliminary answer to the question.

Colours are important indices for Stevens, pointing towards the creation of a certain reality, in this case possibly that of New Haven.[1] The town was indeed constructed by this community, but could it have done this '[w]ithout regard to time or where we are'? The community here is hubristic in its assumption that its members are themselves the foundation for their lives, that their city is made purely of themselves. Aren't these 'colors of the mind' ultimately colours of the sun? And it is worth noting Stevens's use of the first-person plural here: this is, as I pointed out, in contrast to his consideration of the great masses of men in the 1930s and 1940s. It also alerts us that this poem is less about the crises and conquests of the individual Romantic imagination, as some critics would see it, and more concerned with seeing how the shared values of a community are created.

But it is evening and the sun is fading. The colours, whether of the sun or of the mind will soon cede to darkness and what will the town be then? They illuminated the town's existence. The answer that Canto II supposes will not suffice as we find that the houses, 'composed of ourselves', lose their substance – they become 'impalpable habitations', like those of 'The Rock', 'fictional' in the other sense of untrue or unreal. Indeed, Canto III declaims Canto II as wishful thinking: we would like the town and ourselves to exist in a kind of dream and 'move / In the movement of the colors of the mind', but it cannot be. We pray to a hero, Canto III tell us, to make this happen. This canto extends the ideas of both Cantos I and II, firstly, in that it explores the way landscape and more generally space are transformed by human will into fictional spaces (the hero making a 'beau mont'), and secondly, in that it questions how these spaces are founded on some space prior to his will, a raw material, shaped by an agency not his own. We need these transformations and yet at the same time realise their falsity, the way they close us off from the land. The central image with which the canto begins and cryptically ends is the 'hill of stones'. (In the final tercet, the stones of the hill are the bats, the lumps of clay, used to make a piece of porcelain.) We are given the image of 'the hill of stones' existing prior to the agency of the hero, and it is this apprehension of an element of nature, shaped by an agency other than that of the hero's, that makes the 'beau mont' more palpable than the habitations of the previous canto. There is a glimpse here of a way of 'grounding' the human habitations of the city, a way of considering them generically as forces of transformation within and depending on the space of nature. But at this stage it is still merely a glimpse. Like the previous two cantos, Canto III answers the question concerning the composition of the town, in a similar way by locating it with human agency. What made us dream up the town of Canto II? What force makes us construct religions, nations, houses? 'It is', we are told, 'desire, set deep in the eye'. Later, in Canto XXX, this is reversed ('It is not an empty clearness, a bottomless sight'), but much will have happened by that stage to bring Stevens to such an immediate vision of nature. Here its streets, its rooms, the carpets, the walls – in short, the constructed spaces that constitute the town of New Haven – all have their being by virtue of this 'desire, set deep in the eye'. Of course, the physical fact of the town is a result of community's desire for habitations, but Stevens's desideratum is that communities must be *of* the place they inhabit. Their traditions, styles of clothing must give of the land, unlike the jar in Tennessee.

As we move from IV to V, there is a sense of a serious impasse that has yet to be negotiated successfully. The daydream of Canto II had them as 'impalpable' and although this wishful thinking has been discredited the town still floats in a kind of limbo. What now happens is that this insubstantiality spreads outwards, so that in Canto IV even the seasons are distorted by the simplifications of the 'plain men' ('this cold, a children's tale of ice, / Seems like a sheen of heat romanticized'). Canto V holds that such romanticisation is inevitable and depicts the town as walled-in, literally immured in itself, so that it has nothing against which to calibrate its own productions, the spaces that constitute it. In this passage, elements of nature such as lake and ocean can only be seen as subordinate to the constructed space of the house – the lake's reflections inside a room, the ocean lying at the door. There is no sense whatsoever of these elements having an existence that is not based on their adjacency to a human habitation. If we compare this passage to Section IV of 'Extracts', with its freshness and invigoration experienced in the midst of the landscape, its access to reality as something not just of the mind, we register immediately the sense of stiflement here, of wandering through a hall of mirrors. The speaker feels he cannot break out of the encircling mechanics of romanticisation (and thus falsehoods). New Haven becomes: 'A great town hanging pendent in a shade, / An enormous nation happy in a style'.

And yet the speaker knows that he is moving down a blind alley. The reduction to the confines and calibrations of the town alone – as we watch these cantos elaborate one another – increases the sense of claustrophobia, of the town resolutely cloistered within itself, incapable of seeing anything beyond. The canto ends with a kind of creation myth that would explain how matters came to this. The second self utilised that majesty to create its houses, mythologies and nations, but the time has come, as the poem shows, for the self or the community of the town to become *un*happy in 'this style' and try to remember what it left behind in the common earth. If the testimony of this part of the self is heard we shall move closer to making the impalpable habitations more palpable. Nevertheless, we are left with the image of the other part of the self-reaching through earth and sky to find an agency beyond its circumstances. What the first five cantos clearly tell us is that this community of 'selves' will no longer suffice as sovereigns.

Canto VI has been identified by critics as pivotal, but if we remember that the poem is above all a meditation on a town, it then seems like an algebraic aside, something that has to be worked out before returning to the true *materia poetica*, as indeed the poem does in the following canto. In general, critics have ignored the plain fact that Stevens sets out in the poem to say what New Haven is, and is frustrated in this aspiration in the first five cantos because he can find nothing upon which it firmly depends. The question fascinates him as it connected with the questions of community, place, tradition and nature that preoccupied in his other poems. Canto VI is a squabble between the 'custodians of the scene' and it is Canto VII that brings us back to the subject proper of the poem.

Here the demarcation line between humans and their houses is erased: people turn into buildings. The buildings stand for the people, expressing their more everyday thoughts, but also their beliefs and aspirations, their 'conceptions of new mornings of new worlds'. The 'impoverished architects' of this canto could be adherents of the sparse International Style, who, beside the neo-gothic architecture of Yale appear more inventive. In any case, men who have turned into buildings reveal something about themselves that, as human beings, they could keep concealed. I have discussed the way that houses can become spaces representational of a society's belief system. Here Stevens remarks on this aspect as we gain insight into the community's cultural and ethical values, not just into its commonplace facts, by observing its buildings.

In what follows this there is a sense of something new in his consideration of the town, a sense 'Not merely as to the commonplace', a sense that leads beyond the ideas of 'plain men in plain towns'. Looking at the houses of New Haven gives intimations 'as to their miraculous, / Conceptions of new mornings of new worlds'. New Haven was one of the first colonial towns on the continent of America, and in these lines Stevens is able to retrieve part of that sense of colonisation, when the town was enclosed on all sides by a land of which the colonisers were ignorant. While I do not want to say that Stevens engages US history to the same extent as Hart Crane in *The Bridge* or even Williams in *Paterson*, nevertheless, despite some critics' remarks on the arbitrariness of Stevens choice of the town of New Haven (Patke, 217; Berger 92; Bloom, *Wallace Stevens* 306), in the light of such lines we can see that the concerns of the poet of 'The Comedian as the Letter C', in which Crispin arrived as coloniser from Europe, are still current. The lines are strongly suggestive of the time when the town was literally a new haven, or shelter, for the first colonisers of the New World (this colonial past is referred to again in Canto XIX: 'This present colony of a colony / Of colonies'). They also conjure the idea of a space prior to that of the civilisation of the town, a space that at one time enclosed it, and that has now been disregarded.[2]

Canto VIII, voiced like the others in the first-person plural, extends the idea of the community of the town in conversation with something beyond itself, with a woman who is 'the capable / In the midst of foreignness'. In the next chapter I shall show the importance of the experience of the alien: he or she sees more of a land than the indigenes who have become inured to it. We may note also the introduction of the leaves that will feature so strongly later on, especially in Canto XII, and that these are identified with a 'love of the real'. In this canto there is the important moment of leaving the enclosure of the building to experience 'a health of air'. This moment of abandonment of enclosure in favour of the healths of the open air is also very important in many of Stevens's poems. Now as the capable woman appears, we become aware of something 'too imme-diate for any speech', and yet still present. Here the tone is different to that of V: we gain access, through the vision of the alien, to something beyond the precinct of the town. Here also is one of the tiny links of any community – two people talking, with the give and take of question and answer. There is a sense of awed observation of something really substantial, unlike the vision of the dreamy habitations of Canto II.

But what is awe and impassioned cry in VIII is turned to repetition and programme at the beginning of Canto IX. The tone is impatient of twists and turns the poem has taken so far. But even this voice stutters: 'through the certain eye', it says, but then pauses and qualifies this, 'The eye made clear of uncertainty'. The no-nonsense tone modulates smoothly into something very different as the canto moves towards its conclusion. The down-to-earth hotel of the opening is now seen against the vast backdrop of the heavens. That expanse is present in the verse enjambment 'Within it // Everything': the previous statements are precise and measured, even modest in their claims, but then there is a surge against that restraint, a sudden flashflood of desire for the poem of the earth. As we hover over the words 'within it', we expect something careful to follow, a small and bounded statement; what we get is an opening out of spirit beyond the restrictions of the solid town to horizons beyond it. We have to comprehend the plain facts of the town, 'to get as close to the ordinary, the commonplace and the ugly as it is possible for a poet to get', but if this excludes the kind of collective dreamings that every community engages in, then that too is a falsification. We need to attend to the community's sense of the miraculous also, its highest ideals, which make up the metaphysical streets of the physical town.

The next canto explores further this realm of ideal images and beliefs in the heavens. 'Our spirit', it says, is not imprisoned if it admits the solar spectacles of each day as the rhythm of 'our' lives. Here, at last, the sun returns as preceptor and composer of nature, that upon which the town and its inhabitants depend. The approbation with which the word 'hallucinations' is used in this canto indicates that Stevens does not insist on the savage version of 'plain men in plain towns', and will accommodate both plain surface and its hallucination as he answers the question: 'Of what are these houses composed?' Here we are pointed to the cycles of the sun. In Canto XI we are pointed to 'The brilliancy at the central of the earth', thus creating an axis, a golden chain on which the town may be hung.

The giant of Canto I now takes the shape of a 'lion of the spirit', a figure of capable imagination, which is able to produce new 'imaginings' (I) of the town, to *see it as* something else. Harold Bloom holds that lion-shapes follow the man walking around the town, and these irrealities can be dispelled by 'wafts of wakening' (XI) (*Wallace Stevens* 319). I hold that the 'profoundest forms' are the creations of the figure of capable imagination, and that what this canto moves towards is the strongest acknowledgement yet that a majesty beyond that of the most capable spirit is needed as the 'invincible clou' with which to nail down the ontology of the town. The strong rhetorical movement of the canto demotes the agency of humanity and its lions of the imagination, in order to clear a way to something more essential. Comparing these lines beginning 'A verity [. . .]' with those of, say, Canto III, there is a sure sense that the poem has expanded to take in larger horizons. It is like moving from the claustral space of a still life by Chardin to the panoramas of Claude. But the analogy with painting is not completely helpful since in the poem there was a marked need to move outdoors, a need to demote that 'desire, set deep in the eye', in favour of a space that was shaped by agency other than this ocular desire, a 'brilliancy' that radiates from a centre other than the imagination of man.

What occurs then in Canto XII is an attempt to find a cure of the ground as the poet brings together his own articulations with those of nature. The trees stand in by synecdoche for nature, and it is their leaves that are its words, and their shapes when caught by the wind that are its thoughts. As the leaves turn round in 'whirlings in the gutters', the poet is directly faced with an agency other than his own. Stevens often supposes poetry in general as something in which the poet and the written poem merely partake. This could sound like Platonism until we come to the following canto where we realise that there is another poetic agency partaking of this 'poem', that of the utterances of nature, and that this 'poem' cannot come to be without the actions of both the agencies of nature and man. This felicitous interdependence *is* the moment of the poem. Who does Stevens report as speaking in Canto XII? Not only the speaker of the first tercet, but something more. In the first lines, the idea is clear that the poem exists prior to the poet's speaking of it. The sense is that it is disclosed to him as 'part of the res', that he finds it, not that he is sole creator. But he is necessary to it. For some reason this is a privileged moment as the constructed space of the monumental public square loses part of its autonomy and domineering aspect as it gives itself over to the elements of nature – the wind, the trees and the leaves. 'Is' and 'was' are the linguistic instruments that serve the poet as he figures this moment, but 'In the area between is and was are leaves', which are not at his disposal and which manifest an intentionality all of their own: 'leaves in whirlings in the gutters, whirlings / Around and away, resembling the presence of thought'.

The finale of the canto is a confluence of these two agencies: 'words of the world are the life of the world'. Stevens demotes his own figurative powers as a poet in order to leave room for the figurative powers of nature. But what is puzzling is the way that he restrains its final statement with the 'as if' of the penultimate tercet. To dwell on this throws into doubt even Helen Vendler's reading that sees Stevens as salvaging 'a vigorous presence of circulating thought in the wintry scene' (*Extended Wings* 278), since it would seem that the poet only *supposes* that vigorous thought is present. Harold Bloom sees it as the beginning of a movement of 'self-deconstruction' (*Wallace Stevens* 320), but this 'as if' has the effect of renouncing at the last minute any agency that could carry out such deconstruction work and locates all figurative powers firmly within Stevens's own reach. He has taken us to the edge, and at the final moment refused to grant such autonomy to the utterances of nature.

Carried along by the rhythms of the canto we almost miss this two-word phrase, 'as-if', tucked unobtrusively into the corner. Critics genuinely seem to have done so (Berger 96; Bloom, *Wallace Stevens* 319–21; Vendler, *Extended Wings* 276–7), and as a consequence have also missed the thrilling ambivalence of this canto. But at what stage does this ambivalence occur? Only when the leaves, 'the whole psychology, the self, / The town' are conscripted to sing as chorus to the words of the poet. Stevens could be ironising the attempt to make the leaves say what the poet wants. So the possibility of this confluence of agencies is actually indirectly asserted by this restraining 'as if'. A kind of hermeneutic vertigo sets in which a critic attempts to resolve at her or his hazard. And in any case what would be gained? The achievement of this canto is that it brilliantly initiates an interpretive uncertainty that oscillates between different priorities and agencies.

The figure of the poet who was the subject of Canto XII splits into the characters of the ephebe and Professor Eucalyptus in the following two cantos. The difference in their ages echoes lightly with Alpha and Omega of Canto VI, but here the ephebe is also a figure of human imaginative agency. After the rhetorical climax of the preceding canto, there is a definite sense of calm to the next three, as though the fervid ambivalence of XII might be resolved by these two characterisations. And although it seems that the priority of the agency of nature was withheld in Canto XII at the eleventh hour, there remains a sense that it is still imminent. The ephebe walks '[u]nder the birds, among the perilous owls, / In the big x of the returning primitive' (XIII). The uncertainty as to what is returning is conveyed bluntly. In the wake of Canto XII we notice the understated comparison of the eucalyptus tree with the eponymous professor. The appellation of professor in a poem alerts the reader to the possibility of irony. That suspicion is confirmed by the enjambment between the first two tercets, which slyly informs us that the professor, for all his inquisitiveness, is blind. And by virtue of the fact that he is ensconced in his house, his search for reality will not be able to take heed of 'the movable, the moment' (IX). The tree, open to the elements, compares favourably to the professor; the canto tells us that essentially, in the confines of his house, he misses the point. So intent is he on finding 'God in the object itself' that his 'parlance' will not suffice as an 'invincible clou' with which to say what the town is.

Since in both Cantos XIII and XIV one gets the sense that Stevens is disinterestedly working out an intellectual problem, Canto XV is startling as it gains access to what Bloom calls a 'hushed eros, so little credited in Stevens' (*Wallace Stevens* 323). Vestiges of the ironic tone of XIV are still present in this canto's opening, but they fade quickly, and we realise that Stevens's voice has now taken over from that of the Professor – no longer is there a search for God: Canto XV speaks of 'The instinct for earth, for New Haven, for his room'. But despite this modulation of tone, we are still not prepared for the last two startling lines. Let us watch Stevens closely as he negotiates the distance between the irony of the first tercet and the intimate tenderness of the last.

First of all we see how, even in the line just quoted, the conclusion of Canto XI has been fully absorbed as the line moves from a global panorama, then narrows the scope to the town, until it finally arrives in the room. As opposed to the earlier 'desire, set deep in the eye', Stevens now talks of 'instinct', and he shows how this instinct posits 'the brilliancy at the central of the earth' as primordial, against which the room comes to be seen without any irony. What then occurs is that the essence that had not yet been well perceived in Canto XIV, returns so that the 'tink-tonk' of the rain provides the contrapuntal melody to the meditation on this 'instinct for the earth'. Also this rain-melody, by synecdoche, draws the canto outwards to consider what lies beyond the built space of the professor's house. This is what is disclosed. This 'touch' mentioned in the canto is like that of God's to Adam, but it also reminds us of Stevens's earlier meditation on sex, 'Le Monocle de Mon Oncle'. A fantastic balance and ambivalence is achieved here, as due deference is given to the space of nature, the sculpture of its rock, and its seasonal cycles; but also to the power of the 'will', which may transform this space. However these are no blind transformations – the will takes 'trouble' over this, and not only with respect to its own needs. Its hermeneutic practice lifts things literally into the shape of a house, but 'faint' because more knowing, more aware of the horizon of its actions.

The calm sense of reciprocity between the agencies of nature and humanity as they each create their spaces, precipitates the sombre meditation of Canto XVI, where nature is seen as ever-fresh, while that of human imagination eventually ages and stops. The vision of XVI, in which the dilapidation of man's fictional spaces in comparison with the continual newness of nature, creates an anxiety in Stevens as to whether the demotion of constructed habitations has gone too far. In effect, Cantos XVII to XXI mitigate this anxiety, which springs from the sense of imminence in Canto XIII of 'the big x of the returning primitive', which could engulf all man's fictional spaces. A mediation is required.

In Canto XVII this horizon, devoid of habitation for the community or some kind of enclosure, is figured as 'a dominant blank', 'A blank [that] underlies the trials of device'. The town now appears as adjacent or dependent on a space empty of human agency, and the fear is that this space will dominate that of the town. In the face of this horizon, a means is required to allow the community to respond. This amounts to nothing less than a call for a dramatic form. For several communities, including that of the Greeks, tragedy provided such mediation, so that they could endure, as Nietzsche says, 'that overwhelming sense of dismay in the face of the titanic powers of nature, the Moira [Fate] enthroned inexorably over all knowledge, the vulture of the great lover of mankind' (42). But Stevens is neither Nietzsche nor Sophocles: 'The serious reflection is composed / Neither of comic nor tragic but of commonplace'. The robe mentioned, put together from thread, belts and stones, with its fluent movement, answers the metamorphoses of nature. The damask, rippling into one colour from another, responds to this auroral *Moira*. Rajeev Patke remarks in relation to the poem that 'houses, like wigs, hats and clothes, [. . .] are styles of living' (218), and in my reading of the poem 'the robe of rays' becomes an exemplary habitation, one that gives of the space of nature. It is a response that also maintains and protects the space of man's body. If 'the scholar of one candle' of 'The Auroras' had worn such a robe he might have been better prepared to face the Northern Lights.

However, although exemplary, it is hardly practicable and not really commonplace either. It has overtones of old religious ceremonies and cerements. The next canto states this historical difficulty. The window of this canto disallows any return to the Adamic moment when there is no past, when words and things are atoned, and the act of seeing is not mediated by any fiction, be it of painting, or the carpenter's work: we see nature with a modern eye, through window-frames, through the accretions of the past, not with an untrammelled Adamic gaze of wonder.

The carpenter – someone who builds furniture, window frames, and occasionally small suburban houses – is another maker of fictional spaces. Yet another is the 'astral apprentice' referred to later in Canto XVIII, whose constructions are cosmographies with their attendant moralities. The carpenter was present earlier in the form of an architect, a porcelain-maker, the hero who turns the hill of stones into a 'beau mont', the ephebe defining a 'fresh spiritual', the professor of XIV trying to discover divinity in New Haven. The 'fuchsia in a can' is an ironic inversion of the carpenter's situation: the fuchsia, synecdochically a part of nature, is enclosed in a space constructed by man, just as the carpenter and his creations are enclosed by the horizon of nature. *His* iridescences create a city, a city that is eccentric to 'the brilliancy at the central of the earth', and also subject to the dilapidations of time. The town that he creates depends on how things are seen, hermeneutic acts that are so provisional that the city can be 'slapped up like a chest of tools'. His perception, his *seeing-as*, creates the town, which is 'wooden', and the 'astral apprentices' build their systems on this model. We are left with 'eccentric exteriors' rather than being brought directly by the carpenter to the 'central of the earth'. For, he is a maker of fictions, be they 'wooden', and these mediate our relationship with the 'central'. We are enclosed by his fictions, distanced from the horizon of nature, sheltered from the elements, just as the fictions of the cosmic apprentice fill the metaphysical void of belief. Terrestrial and astral apprentices conspire to protect us, but in the process draw us further away from our sources of imaginative strength.

Canto XIX circles the ideal of a hero, 'a figure like Ecclesiast', one who would provide a cure for the eccentricity of the town, this configuration on the outer radial regions of another centre. His mediation is necessary, but he must be, as the figure of XX is not, cognisant of both 'clouds and men'. The distinction between men and their houses is erased, and the figure of capable imagination is called upon to mediate the relationship between architecture and nature. But this architecture, this living in rooms, breeds the cowardice that – horrified by the 'dilapidation of dilapidations' (XVI) – forces him to retreat inside himself to where his imaginary projects encounter no friction. What is ironic about this, as Stevens points out, is that even such dreaming is housed and placed against huge horizons, against Nietzsche's *Moira*, that for which the wind and trees stand in synecdochically. The hero that this canto demands is one who can make an 'alternate romanza // Out of the surfaces, the windows, the walls, / The bricks grown brittle in time's poverty, / The clear'. This 'celestial mode' referred to in this canto cannot be provided by the figure of Canto XX because he is immured in the building. He refuses to 'descend to the street and inhale a health of air' (VIII). Instead he 'sits thinking in the corners of a room' much like those rationalists of 'Six Significant Landscapes' who would never dream of swapping their mortar boards for sombreros.

The wind's voice in Canto XXI that brings together the 'two romanzas' carries down through Canto XXII, albeit in another allotrope. That Stevens talks of nature as 'romanza' indicates how nature is always *seen as* something by humanity, no matter how epistemologically pure the questor is. The poem is haunted by the traces of a campagna that is cleared of human interpretation: it wants to behold the Nietzschean *Moira* emerging without mediation before the attentive eye. But this need is countered by the knowledge that such Adamic aspirations can never be fulfilled.

At some stage during a reading of the poem, every reader will nod in agreement with Stevens's own description of 'An Ordinary Evening' as 'endlessly elaborating' (XXVIII). As I read it here, I am following the troughs and nodes of crisis, exaltation and resolution, only for these same patterns to begin again a canto later. The poem of course resolves nothing, or if it does, the resolution must be repeated very soon again. Its elaborations are a kind of parody of the pattern of crisis and resolution, as though Stevens is saying that to live in a place is to engage constantly in such thought. But beneath all this to-ing and fro-ing of the meditating mind, there is a general undercurrent that sweeps us out to the surrounding expanses of nature, which registers Stevens's ultimate dissatisfaction with being ensconced in the space of the town. His nature is difficult to apprehend, hard to get at, fleeting when it does appear, but it is the base for his thought on human community, its habitations and dreamings.

Returning to the Adamic aspirations, Wordsworth's desire 'to see into the heart of things' is similar. Having left his friends behind, he wanders alone until he comes upon the intense revelation on top of Mount Snowdon (Wordsworth 510, 512). *The Prelude* records moments such as these with an innate knowledge of their absolute priority for human existence, but without attempting to relate the sense of access to nature, which he gained on the mountain top, to the expanses appropriated by our towns. This distance from human habitations and company is perhaps what vouchsafes them for Wordsworth. Although Stevens also feels this Wordsworthian need for revelation (viz., the impatient tone of the opening lines of IX), he rejects the stance of the English poet: 'Creation is not renewed by images / Of lone wanderers' (XXII). In Stevens, and especially in 'An Ordinary Evening', the Romantic interview is often between architecture and nature. This complication of the Romantic sublime is crucial to our awareness of Stevens as an inheritor *and* transformer of that tradition. The difficult task of the poem is to broker a relationship, not between some 'lone wanderer' and a hilltop panorama, but between a community and the space of nature. Nature is a plastic force itself, and Stevens, in the poem, investigates the phases of the difference between nature as a plastic force and between the community of the poem that has effected its own transformations on the land over the last few centuries. This is an American twist to the Romantic sublime of the English poet that takes cognisance of the history of the place. He must ask: 'What is the radial aspect of this place'? And he knows that the answer will be different because the community of this town have had a different relationship to the landscape and nature of the place to that of Wordsworth and his community (or lack of it, at least on top of Mount Snowdon). This is why 'images of lone wanderers' will not suffice in New Haven. This is why Stevens's sublime is signally different.

The wind of Canto XXI as that which unites 'the distant and the near' finds its scion in XXII in 'the *inhalations* of original cold / And of original earliness' (italics mine). The star is yet another synecdochic substitute for nature, on this occasion as the best example of 'the distant'. The breath (ψυχή) of the poet reproduces the *psyche* of the wind, as he searches for a way to mediate between 'the distant and the near'. This is similar to the reflection of the 'robe of rays'. Up to now, nature has only been hinted at synecdochically through images of the sun, the moon, the wind, the green ferns, the rain 'falling loudly in trees / And on the ground', but in the final lines of Canto XXIV, as Stevens refers to the demise of the Greek gods, we see how the town, at the crucial moment of the disappearance of the gods, depends on it for its existence. This is like the movement towards the surrounding landscape in 'Sunday Morning'. What is noticeable is that Stevens figures the annihilation of Jove in spatial terms – to smash the icon is to smash the god. ('There is no difference between god and his temple' [OP 191].) In other words, if things such as gods do not have spatial existence, they do not exist at all. Space with its bodies and relations is whence all metaphysics emerges. The disappearance of Jove is a call to interpret space once more, to build once again, but this time without repeating the previous forms. There must be an escape from repetition. Stevens lingers on this initial moment of incipient human action. There is a 'clearing', a call to see things once again.

'To see the gods dispelled in mid-air and dissolve like clouds is one of the great human experiences. [. . .] It left us feeling dispossessed and alone in a solitude, like children without parents, in a home that seemed deserted, in which the amical rooms and halls had taken on a look of hardness and emptiness' (OP 260). It then becomes the job of poetry to search again for ways to see the house and town. With Jove's statue and its like exploded, the poet must ask questions such as those of Cantos I to V, which suppose that human control was supreme. However, what fascinates Stevens here is the moment that precedes the hermeneutic act. He lingers over this interpretive blankness, knowing that it cannot endure, but nevertheless asserting its importance as the space that precedes all human making. He prolongs this blankness by talking of fiction-making in the most abstract of terms. Bloom curtly dismisses this canto and Vendler ignores it, preferring instead to dwell on Canto XXV. And yet here with an increased scope and awareness, we are brought back to the central questions of the poem. How is the town to be seen? What upholds it? Of what is it composed? The clearing of the gods, be they Christian or Greek, lever the town into a position where it is seen against the horizon. It is 'poised' there, conveying the idea of a set of force fields that are completely new and different from the hypostases of the gods. They are poised about 'the brilliant central' of the earth.

Nature appears in this 'clearing' but will be romanticised in Canto XXVI and 'seen as inamorata'. However, the hidalgo of Canto XXV appears as the figure who might maintain this vision of nature free of any *seeing-as*. He is like the figure of the indigene, which I shall discuss in the next chapter, but for now I shall just remark that while such figures exert a fascination for Stevens, with their osmotic relationship with their land, he ultimately cannot be satisfied with them and their 'man-locked set'. The hidalgo fails and in Canto XXVI 'romanzas' are conjured once again. What is significant is the turn here from the town to the surrounding landscape. No critic has remarked on the way that poem begins immured in the town and then draws out toward the countryside, initiating a whole new set of angles and perspectives. Charles Berger says that '"Ordinary Evening" is urban where "Credences" is pastoral' (90). But why then, if he is discussing an ordinary in New Haven city, does he consider the landscape of XXX, and why, in XXVI, does he move from looking at the sidewalk to the larger horizon of the landscape of the eastern coastline and the sound that separates the town from Long Island? The sun moving through the sky conjures fluent chiaroscuros and strange colours out of the ordinary town, and the landscape that surrounds it. This is like the colour metamorphoses that Hartford undergoes in the purple light (CP 226–7). Stevens employs one of his favourite moves of reducing objects to their colour components. And although he rejects the lush Fauvism that figures nature as inamorata, what is noteworthy is the sense of panorama in this canto. We move outward to the capes and the nearby sound. This access to the wider land- and seascapes of Connecticut follows the demolition of Jove in Canto XXIV, when we saw the 'town poised at the horizon's dip', and it is in the more general context of Stevens's poetry a move to view humanity and its social forms against the background of landscape and nature.

Although in the earlier shorter version of the poem (in the *Selected Poems*) the order of the last four cantos was different, it is helpful to see a dialectic movement here in Cantos XXVIII, XXIX, and XXX: Canto XXVIII deals with the relationship of the town to the metaphorical construals of the poet – it is *seen as* one thing or another; XXIX, in its anecdotal way, deals with the same issue, but this time against the larger horizon of nature; XXX, then, with its measured and decidedly un-anecdotal tone, represents the full emergence of the horizon of nature, cleared of human metaphors, the 'stiff and stubborn, man-locked set'. Stevens indicates this by juxtaposing XXX with the stylised tone of XXIX, where he harks back to a more ludic attitude towards language. The consequent emergence of the cool descriptive lines of XXX then mimics the emergence of nature into the awareness of the poet. Harold Bloom says that 'we experience a great sense of liberation [in XXX] when we are told: "A clearness has returned. Its stands restored"' (*Wallace Stevens* 335).

With the liberating light that XXX throws back along the poem, how can we rest easy with Canto XXVIII as a description of reality? Bloom says of this canto: 'On the premise that reality has been taken up into the mind, that the First Ideas of nature, other persons, art, and one's own body have been re-imagined fully, then it follows at last that real and unreal, reduction and expansion, are two in one' (*Wallace Stevens* 331). But what is remarkable to me about the first lines of XXVIII, especially after we have been brought by Stevens past huge horizons of weather and landscape, is their proposal that 'reality' in its fullness is anything so confined. If Stevens entertained Fauvism in XXVI, then here he becomes a still-life painter, perhaps one like Jean-Baptiste-Siméon Chardin. The first tercet describes a conflation of that artist's two companion still lifes, *The Brioche* and

Grape and Pomegranates. Without doubt there is a need at this stage in such a long poem for the respite from searching that 'her // Misericordia' provide, but we have not come so far to settle only for the closeted space of eighteenth-century French painting. This sense of confinement is followed through in the second and third tercets as cities are ridiculously reduced to *vedute* and conversational asides, Stevens thus ironically undercutting the proposal of the first tercet.

But the irony in this case is not fully condemnatory, since Stevens goes on to say that at least some vestige of these cities is maintained by these *vedute*, whereas 'A more severe, // More harassing master' would retain no vestige of the real cities as he went on to create the 'heavens, the hells, the worlds, the longed-for lands'. So, although he is aware of the (literal) limitations of viewing reality in such confined ways, it is as if he is fearful of expanding his scope lest metaphor becomes the instrument of a will-to-power, a will to transform the world violently through 'the intricate evasions of as'. This restraint does not arise from any simplistic moral scruple, but rather from the feeling that that such an 'evasion' would not adhere to the 'commonplace', which is the project of the poem.

That Stevens is not that more severe and harassing master is abundantly evident from the playful stylisation of the next canto. The change of mode (from meditative tone to stylised anecdote) is strange, whereas in 'Notes' such jumps were the norm. The theme is how collective imaginings change reality, but qualifies this change as a change of adjective not substantive. Here the troping power of humanity is characterised by what it does to the land and its vegetation. The two lands of the canto permeate human speech, creating an osmotic relationship between the people and their place. These communities – their speech, their tradition – give of the place they inhabit, and it is the mariners, travelling between the two lands who are able to observe this most clearly. The respite from staring hard at ordinary New Haven, which this passage provides, allows him to reassess the relation between language and nature. They are interdependent – the sharp *r*-sound mimes the sharp taste of the lemon, the words of the people of the place are described as autochthonous. What happens to the mariners when they travel to a different land is that they encounter a language with different adjectives that describe a different physical reality.

Such a swapping of adjectives could appear trivial but in the portentous stylisation of this canto, it is a significant demonstration, an index that nature is prior to the enclosures, be they aesthetic or social, that man creates. An indication

> that we live in a place
> That is not our own and, much more, not ourselves
> And hard it is in spite of blazoned days.
>
> We are the mimics. Clouds are pedagogues
> The air is not a mirror but bare board,
> Coulisse bright-dark, tragic chiaroscuro

And comic color of the rose, in which
Abysmal instruments make sounds like pips
Of the sweeping meanings that we add to them.   (CP 383–4)

What happens in Canto XXX is Stevens attempts to provide a vision of that place that is not our own: 'Poetry has to be something more than a conception of the mind. It has to be a revelation of nature' (OP 191). When he says '[i]t is a coming on and a coming forth', the verbs' subject is not human. This at last is the 'reality' upon which all human fictions depend, whether they be nation states, cities, towns – it is the troping space of nature. This is not then a passive landscape, a painting by Ruisdael hanging on a wall, or Bergamo in a postcard, but that which has an agency that contains all the agencies of man, which tropes before man. The eyes could be those of the animals, who are the denizens of nature. Or it could be the 'one mind' of the human individual facing this nature unsheltered by any enclosure. He sees the seeing of the animals. And also it could be that he is a representative of the community and the eyes of humanity see through his as the poem finally reveals itself. This is a more communal version of the million people on one string of 'The Man with the Blue Guitar'. This clearness has returned after the enclosures of the beginning of the poem have been breached. Here we face out into nature, and the sense of access and scope is palpable: the tone and movement of the canto, as Stevens moves through the landscape, are purely positive, and this access and this scope cannot be experienced within the space of the city – it is to nature that he must turn.

The effort to get at this clarity is the same as the effort to 'get at' (XXXI) the existence of the town. Charged with the force of this knowledge, the final canto dizzily reviews the whole poem and its contents. It is an afterthought, an addendum, whose high theoretical pitch is won for brief seconds by the dialectic movement of cantos XXVIII, XXIX and XXX. The last two sentences are spoken by a voice that is running out of oxygen, and which desperately tries to conclude but won't or can't. The first three tercets make a hurried reprise of the poem's concerns, with images that play between phenomena and their causes (the men that made the town, the sheets that score the thunder). The candle burning before the sea makes us imagine the fire-foam of the waves, and confirms that there is no end run to ultimate causes, of the town, the thunder, or the fire in the sea. The process of working out such connections demands 'edgings and inchings', and also leads to a consideration not only of the surrounding spaces but also of the long course of history from Constantine to the latest American president. A lot of the poem was concerned with the collective mythology of the townspeople, their sense of the miraculous as well as their commonplace, and such a political figure occupies something of a middle ground between these two poles. The president is an expression of collective desire, and so characterises the people as did the architects of Canto VII. But approaching this desire and the forms it takes, Stevens, as I have shown, repeatedly must turn to calibrate it against natural

109

phenomena – the sun, the moon, the seasons, the surrounding land- and seascapes. That one lives in a land that has been ruled up to very recently by a particular president changes your perception of things, and thus the course of history from Constantine to the present is also the evolution of human perception.

The fourth and fifth tercets tell us that the search for a form, a fiction, a space within the horizon of nature, will never conclude, and after coming so far we are left only with an optative. But it is an optative in which the town and its community hover in mid-air, with matters of agency and decision left uncertain. Insofar as it rejects the limitations of a solid body (strictly delimited space, say, that of the town and its houses) and chooses a trope of light and movement, it sums up the fluent attitude of the poem as a whole, as it moved from the fertile investigation of the confines of the imagination in Cantos I to V, through the ever-widening horizons from VI to XI where it arrives at an intimation of 'the brilliancy at the central of the earth' – then to the testing of the different hermeneutic paths of the ephebe and the professor. Once it had evolved an attitude from these two, it had to negotiate the temporal anxieties of XVI. Cantos XXIII and XXIV figured an enclosure within a larger space, and the clearing in which nature emerges is glimpsed in XXIV and then consolidated after the dialectic movement of XXVIII, XXIX and XXX. It is a fluency of attitude that allows the poem to 'get at' such horizons and see that New Haven, standing in for all human making, is nothing if the horizon of nature is excised from our vision; we must be adept in recognising forces and agencies in the midst of shadows and night. Many poets when they reach the end of their career move toward thesis, fixity, credo. Stevens refuses this for uncertainty, fluency, possibility, shown in his very choice of the conditional form a verb to end one of his longest and most important poems; determination and agency recede into ghosthood. In the middle of New Haven, fully comprehending the natural horizon stretching out around and above it, a clearness returns '[i]n which hundreds of eyes, in one mind, see at once'.

Chapter 5

Family, nation, race

The affectionate emigrant found
A new reality in parrot-squawks.

– 'The Comedian as the Letter C'

1

In the phase of his career from roughly 1942 to his death, nature in Stevens's poetry was increasingly connected with ideas of family, community and nation. Most of the poems of this period are voiced in the first-person plural, as distinct from the individual figures of the earlier work. It can be no accident that the earlier work was also full of images of nature and landscape as they floated free of ideological constructs, or, as he has it in 'Angel without Paysans', of their 'man-locked set'. An index of this is his use of Pennsylvania and New Jersey place names that appear in the poems of the mid-1940s. They mark an important shift in his thinking, and this shift has been passed over by his readers so far.[1] In his previous poems, the imagination, despite its vicissitudes, has no genealogy: its grandeurs and nadirs are of its own making; it owes nothing to past generations; if strong enough, it has the power to recreate the world; it would seem to have sprung like Jay Gatsby 'from his Platonic conception of himself' (Fitzgerald 95). But in the phase of his career after the writing of 'Notes Toward a Supreme Fiction' (1942), such an Emersonian conception of the imagination is abandoned, and in its place there is an awareness of the imagination as *scion*, that is, as the product of many generations which have dwelled in specific places. Moreover, contrary to the pervasive Emersonian prejudice, this awareness is figured in the poetry as an access to clear vision and imaginative power, Stevens's two great desiderata. It is little wonder that this shift has gone unnoticed: such a conception of imaginative inheritance and maturity goes against deeply held beliefs of self-determination which are integral to US democratic ideology (and indeed which are increasingly to be found in Anglophone countries and Europe). For Stevens, the production of imaginative nobility begins to resemble the production of nobility in feudal Europe, rather than that of the 'natural nobility' promoted by American writers as diverse as Walt Whitman and Henry James.

Milton J. Bates holds that Stevens's genealogical studies confirmed rather than challenged his conception of the imagination and reality:

> Along with physique and temperament, Stevens believed that he had inherited certain of his poetic preoccupations. His 'reality-imagination complex' was, he asserted in 1953, uniquely his own (L 792). But it was also a latter-day version of complementary instincts which had informed his ancestors' lives – their belief in God and their attachment to the soil. (283)

He goes on to assert that his ancestors, and especially the figure of his maternal grandfather, 'moved Stevens to project a supreme fiction or central poem in the forties and fifties' (285). But this will not do, as Stevens drops all talk of supreme fictions after 1942, and in its place, as I shall show, there is a more circumspect filial piety towards tradition and the past. Alan Filreis comes closer to an awareness of the importance of the shift ('genealogy offered him not only a lesson in the content of these centuries-old political disputes, but also taught him a method of unraveling positions within positions' [*Actual World* 123]), but his emphasis on the connections between the poetry and politics means that he only dwells on the implications of the interest for Stevens's thinking about World War II.

Since this idea – that respect for family tradition and place is the way to a clear perception of the world – is uncommon, it must be stressed that such filial piety is in no way an instance of imaginative cowardice or dependence, but is for Stevens the imagination's very ennobling and empowerment.

When W. B. Yeats writes 'Under Ben Bulben', he locates himself in a region that many of his preceding poems have mapped out imaginatively, connecting it not only with his family history but the fate of Ireland in general. Stevens's references to Tinicum, Cohansey, Tulpehocken, and the Perkiomen Creek, have a very different effect. These places are not charged with the same representational value as the plateau in County Sligo; in fact, their very lack of national signifi-cance seems to have been part of the motivation for their choice. Looking to the letters, we can obtain glosses on them, and these are excellently supplemented by Bates (277–86). We learn that when tracing his genealogy in the period, Stevens discovered that his ancestors lived in some of these places. Others places are even more immediate: for instance, of the Perkiomen Creek he remarked: 'It almost amounts to a genealogical fact that all his life long my father used to fish in Perkiomen for bass, and this can only mean that he did it as a boy' (SP 5). Once we know this, and once we know of Stevens's troubled relationship with his father, the poem's emotional charge is greatly increased.

And yet it is hard not to suspect that he was uninterested in such an effect: if he had been why did he not make the connection between his father and the stream more obvious? It seems unlikely that he wished to lead the reader on a paper chase for the fact. In February 1942, just before he embarked on these poems, he gave his opinion on poetic obscurity to Hi Simons:

> Sometimes, when I am writing a thing, it is complete in my own mind; I write it in my own way and don't care what happens. I don't mean to say that I am deliberately obscure, but I do mean to say that, when the thing has been put down and is complete to my own way of thinking, I let it go. After all, if the thing is really there, the reader gets it. He may not get it at once, but, if he is sufficiently interested, he invariably gets it. (L 403)

'Sufficient interest' probably doesn't stretch to *Souvenirs and Prophecies*, from which I took the reference to his father – that is scholarly interest. But it probably does stretch to knowing that Stevens was from Pennsylvania, and inferring from this that the place names had a family resonance for him. Then the reader begins to 'get it'. He or she will be ushered further in this direction by the many references to both family relations and the passage of generations in these poems. (Bates remarks on the increased use of familial terms in this period [277ff].)

The first important poem of this phase is 'Dutch Graves in Bucks County' (1943), and in it he marks the distance between the past generations and the present moment. The Dutch ancestors in the ground 'are crusts that lie / In the shrivellings of your time and place' (CP 291) and Stevens tells them that 'your children are not your children' (CP 292). This is the most heartbreaking consequence of emigration – the breakdown in the transmission of culture and language. Stevens addresses them throughout the poem as his 'semblables' and it is hard not to recall his own difficulties with his daughter at that time. Writing to his sister in October 1942, Stevens takes stock of Holly's growing distance from him and his family, even while he expresses understanding of it (L 421). Holly herself when editing the letters suggests that her break with her parents was one of the reasons for his interest in genealogy (L 398). Almost a year to the day later he writes to Hi Simons about his interest in it:

> This was a subject that I scorned when I was a boy. However, there has become a part of it something that was beyond then and that is the desire to realize the past as it was. At the moment I am reading a history of the early settlements which in a perfectly effortless way recreates the political tensions and the business activity of the 17th century in this country. This is an extraordinary experience, and the whole thing has been an extraordinary experience: finding out about my family, etc. (L 457)

In this context 'Dutch Graves', although first published in 1943, belongs to the first period of genealogical research as Stevens describes it. It is as if the attainment of the second phase had not yet penetrated Stevens's poetic imagination – the poems resulting from that would follow soon. In the meantime, 'So-And-So Reclining on Her Couch' examines the advertising spectacle of a woman who would seem to have been born 'at twenty-one // Without lineage or language, only / The curving of her hip [. . .]' (CP 295). Just as *The Great Gatsby* in part hinges on the revelation of Gatbsy's true past with the arrival of his father at the end of the book, so does Stevens's poem reveal both the lineage and language of the apparitional beauty that floats before his eyes. Waving her away dismissively at the end, he says: 'Good-bye, / Mrs. Pappadopoulos, and thanks' (CP 296). Given the stately philosophical rhetoric of the rest of the poem, it is clear that Stevens has chosen the multisyllabic Greek name for comic effect: her ethnic background, which either she or the advertisers had endeavoured to erase, cannot be suppressed. The poem, although it amounts to little more than a comic fillip, marks a movement away from the position of the stentorian 'Dutch Graves': Mrs Pappadopoulous, much as she would wish it, cannot prevent the past being part of the present.

Lineage and language are exactly what the speaker of 'Debris of Life and Mind' desires most: 'There is so little that is close and warm. / It is as if we were never children' (CP 338). In this absence he imagines a maternal figure who comes forth to console him, and reassure him about himself and the things of the world. She is referred to in the third person throughout the brief lyric, and this makes the last line so poignant when he turns to address her directly: 'Stay here. Speak of familiar things a while' (CP 338). The knot of meanings in the word 'familiar' is particularly evocative: in one sense these things are the objects we know best, in another, they pertain to one's family or household. Writing to Emma Stevens Jobbins in 1944 he joked: 'It is such a pleasure to hear from you. In the autumn I badly need my mother, or something. This has always been the toughest time of the year for me [. . .]' (L 473). Through the joke shimmers something of the feeling of 'Debris' – after all, it is a strange way for a man of 65 to begin a letter to a relation. In the same year he published 'Esthétique du Mal'; in section V (CP 317) he stresses the need for family as antidote in part to evil:

> For this familiar,
> This brother even in the father's eye,
> This brother half-spoken in the mother's throat
> And these regalia, these things disclosed,
> These nebulous brilliancies in the smallest look
> Of the being's deepest darling, we forego
> Lament, willingly forfeit the ai-ai.

What is 'close and warm' in 'Debris of Life and Mind' is present again in the 'familiar things' of 'the actual, the warm, the near'. Also of note is the way Stevens figures such intimacy as access to the real: there is the aforementioned 'actual' and the disclosure later on in the passage. (Ideas of 'disclosure' are important to

Stevens in this period and the word occurs repeatedly in the poems.) Section XIII begins with fathers and sons and considers the central role of lineage in the conception and perception of the world. One follows the other and each in his being is unalterable. Stevens glosses this in the passage beginning 'This force of nature in action [. . .]' (CP 324). The man reclining in the Mediterranean cloister is some relation to Mrs Pappadopoulos: the tone seems to imply that it's all very well for some expatriate meditating in a cloister away from home and family (viz., the figure of Section I), engaged in such activities as 'establishing the visible'. But to those who remain at home and aware of their place in the generations a grimmer fate awaits. Here Stevens explores the meaning of 'familiar' as enemy or assassin, but for all the inimical nature of this figure, it is clear that approbation is reserved for those who confront the disclosure of the assassin. The 'blood' of the last line is at once the liquid and the lineage of the individual. One feels one's father moving in one's blood. From family he moves outwards to social organisation in Section XIV, and then there is final section, XV, 'The greatest poverty is not to live [. . .]'. I have discussed the importance of the linkage between XIV and XV in Chapter Two, but here I would like to stress how integral in the overall context of the poem are the 'familiar disclosures' of earlier sections to the access to the physical world in XV (CP 325–6). If one does not feel the action of generations 'moving in the blood' then one cannot 'get at' the experience of the physical world which is so beautifully evoked in the final section.

Perhaps,

After death, the non-physical people, in paradise,
Itself non-physical, may, by chance, observe
The green corn gleaming and experience
The minor of what we feel. The adventurer
In humanity has not conceived of a race
Completely physical in a physical world.
The green corn gleams and the metaphysicals
Lie sprawling in majors of the August heat,
The rotund emotions, paradise unknown.
This is the thesis scrivened in delight,
The reverberating psalm, the right chorale.

The ghosts of past generations are like those of 'Large Red Man Reading' who come back down to earth, and that Stevens wishes us to connect the passage with 'familiar things' is clear from his mention of the 'adventurer' which reminds us of the 'adventure to be endured' of XIII. That we can never perceive the world in a purely physical way is put down to the fact that in our blood the non-physical people still move, so that when we look over the gleaming corn they seem to lie there as part of it. We should attend to the movement of approbation in the passage. Rather than supposing that the presence of the dead generations in vision is harmful or limiting, in the last two lines above he celebrates them joyously.

Confirmation of the importance of the family figures to clear vision is provided by the 'The Bed of Old John Zeller', which follows immediately in the *Collected Poems*. The first tercet picks up the theme of evil and 'ghostly sequences' of the generations. One might get frustrated that one's vision of the world is conditioned by one's ancestors and this might push one to imagine a different lineage. If one feels thus, then one begins to think that something may replace it. Zeller (1809–62), Stevens's maternal grandfather, was born in Berks County and died in Reading (L 416), and here he calls his grandson away from mere invention of supreme fictions to the hard work of the recognition of reality. The recommendation is that the 'structure of ideas' should 'accept the structure / Of things', and this clearly demotes the action of the sovereign imagination in its projection of supreme fictions in favour of the disclosure of reality. One must 'feel this action in the blood' to reach such a disclosure, as we saw in 'Esthétique du Mal'. While this is hardly one of Stevens's most impressive poems, it serves as a valuable index to what is going on in a more important work such as 'Credences of Summer'.

But before approaching this poem, I give a few other indexes to the theme of family and tradition, and occasionally place. 'The Lack of Repose' makes further 'intense disclosures' (CP 303) encouraged by an awareness of the passage of generations, and sees these proleptically rather than retrospectively. The speaker imagines his grandson some time in the future taking strength and understanding from the book he has yet to write. Such praise of lineage is the corollary of 'So-And-So Reclining on Her Couch'. Similarly, 'Sketch of Ultimate Politician' dwells on words 'That have rankled for many lives and made no sound' (CP 336) which, when spoken by this figure, create the land in which the community will soon live. 'Somnabulisma' considers the different metaphors for the sea of successive generations. The syntax is complex, but finally through negative implication asserts the desideratum of a connection between a people and their place through the mediation of a scholar figure. 'Wild Ducks, People and Distances' expresses something of the claustrophobia of this connection ('We grew used so soon, too soon, to earth itself [. . .]' [CP 328]). We might have wished for the easy option outlined in 'The Bed of Old John Zeller' ('Did we expect to live in other lives?' [CP 328]), but the poem ends by affirming the value of the villages: there remains a distance between us and where we live, but to close that gap would be fatal. Locating himself back in Pennsylvania in 'Late Hymn from the Myrrh-Mountain', he experiences a moment of nearness with the external world – the distance of 'Wild Ducks' closed a little, but not entirely. 'Thinking of a Relation Between the Images of Metaphors' is concerned with another accord with reality through parentalia, that is, ceremonious acknow-ledgement of a parent. Stevens's father, fishing in the Perkiomen Creek, provides access to a further 'disclosure': 'State the disclosure. In that one eye the dove /

Might spring to sight and yet remain a dove. // The fisherman might be that single man / In whose breast, the dove, alighting, would grow still' (CP 357).

One would suppose that 'A Completely New Set of Objects' (CP 352–3) would result from ignoring ancestors, but Stevens turns this supposition on its head. Regarding the place names in the penultimate line of the poem, Holly Stevens comments that 'Stevens had sought information regarding his father's side of the family in these cemeteries' (L 290). What seems at first like a surreal procession turns out to be based on a memory of similar events on the Schuylkill in Reading. In the Wallace Stevens Memorial Issue of the *Historical Review of Berks County*, Donald Shenton offers this gloss:

> In 1897 the Schuylkill had been damned at frequent intervals to provide a channel deep enough for boats of Schuylkill Canal, which carried coal from the north to Philadelphia. Thus the river had impressive breadth. Then annual festivals were held on this broad river, down which paraded canoes and boats lighted at night with candled Chinese lanterns. Oldsters, remembering these festivals, will enjoy 'A Completely New Set of Objects' (page 107), as they envision with Stevens the lighted canoes emerging from the curtain of night as if 'from mid-earth' – first the light, then the dim shapes of canoes, then the faces of old friends reappearing out of the night of memory.

He extends this memory to say that the people emerge from mid-earth, making them an autochthonous community, *of* the place they reside in. These figures, instead of restricting our apprehension of the world, expand it – only by attending to a community's traditions will one come to know that community's place. The tone of this, intimate and affectionate, could not be further removed from that of 'Dutch Graves' written three years before. Neither is there any suggestion of a supreme fiction. The speaker is carrying out his loving and dutiful parentalia: he is a 'beholder', not a projector of some grand plan. Here is the sense of harmony referred to at the end of 'Extraordinary References', which is set in Tulpehocken where his mother's family once lived: 'In the inherited garden, a second-hand / Vertumnus creates an equilibrium' (CP 369).

Primed with by such readings, our awareness of a poem like 'The Red Fern' (CP 365) is transformed, and we see how deeply Stevens's genealogical research has changed his imagination, and how deeply it is the vision of a lyric subject that is embedded in the levels of generation rather than the pastless Emersonian individual. That the clouds are 'less firm' than the fern is an ingenious rhyme. But even more impressive is the way that Stevens throws open the scope of the poem in the last verse, so that observation of the fern becomes a parable embracing the generations of men as well as that of the fern. The infant, in his relation to the fatherly figure that addresses him, is one of those 'reflections and off-shoots, mimic-motes'. The implication is that a person cannot pierce the physical fix of things until he or she learns to see through such 'familiar' resemblances. The last stanza thus contrasts two types of vision: the first a childish inventory of the objects of the world, the second much more penetrating and alive, and the verve of this second is conveyed on a phonetic level by the effervescence of the words 'physical fix'. But of course this is not just an awareness of resemblances in the world – if that were all, then the individual imagination would be capable of that – but rather it is an awareness that one is also a reflection or off shoot from the 'furiously burning father-fire'; in other words, that one is a scion and sees in that way.

What could be further from Emerson, who when walking through the countryside experiencing his revelation of the universe declared that at that moment the 'name of the nearest friend sounds then foreign and accidental: to be brothers, to be acquaintances, master or servant, is then a trifle and a distur-bance' (6)? The exultant, aggressive tone of Canto II of 'Credences of Summer' is very similar to Emerson's in *Nature* (1836). In it he exclaims:

> Let's see the very thing and nothing else.
> Let's see it with the hottest fire of sight.
> Burn everything not part of it to ash.   (CP 373)

But now we begin to realise that Stevens's access to reality in such moments rather than depending on the abandonment of the ties of family and intimate acquaintance, depend on them, and acknowledge their importance. How else should we understand canto I, especially its last verse?

> There is nothing more inscribed nor thought nor felt
> And this must comfort the heart's core against
> Its false disasters – these fathers standing round,
> These mothers touching, speaking, being near,
> These lovers waiting in the soft dry grass.   (CP 372)

Stevens has moved from the consideration of the great masses of men which preoccupied him through the 1930s into the early 1940s, to a consideration of community, with its ceremonies, family ties, and transmission of cultural and ethical values. Great masses of men possess none of these attributes: the very phrase conjures up populations that have no cultural or ethical values but those the radio and newspapers give them; they are populations of individual economic units without brothers, sisters, parents, lovers, without the ability to apprehend the kind of negotiations with the sun, the moon, the mountains and the sea that the poet conducts. In the passage above, and indeed in the poem in general, Stevens is able to give a sense of large numbers of people caught up in the cycle of birth, love and death, but also something of the warmth and intensity of the human emotions that cathect this process. Observe the last three lines: the fathers stand around sternly as though posing for a family photograph; the mothers with their tenderness break this mood as they touch, speak and simply draw near; and the description of the lovers conveys the *luxus* and lyricism of young love. These emotions are registered, but also placed against the larger backdrop of the generational cycles of the community. Each element of this picture has a social role – these are the 'personae' mentioned in the last section of the poem.

Confirming this reading is the setting of Canto IV in Oley:

> One of the limits of reality
> Presents itself in Oley when the hay,
> Baked through long days, is piled in mows. It is
> A land too ripe for enigmas, too serene.
> There the distant fails the clairvoyant eye
>
> And the secondary senses of the ear
> Swarm, not with secondary sounds, but choirs,
> Not evocations but last choirs, last sounds
> With nothing else compounded, carried full,
> Pure rhetoric of a language without words.
>
> Things stop in that direction and since they stop
> The direction stops and we accept what is
> As good. The utmost must be good and is
> And is our fortune and honey hived in the trees
> And mingling of colors at a festival.

This landscape has already been woven through with social meaning by the generations of the people who have lived here: the 'secondary sounds' that are to be heard in Oley are those of the choirs of the community whose songs have become part of the place. That Stevens had this socio-historical aspect of the land-scape in mind is confirmed by his letter to Charles Tomlinson when he comments:

> Oley (Óly), by the way, is a region in eastern Pennsylvania. It is a valley full of farms which was settled in part by Huguenots in the 17th Century. An accord with realities is the nature of things there. (L 719)

When we know these things, the lines, 'One of the limits of reality / Presents itself in Oley', take on a special resonance. The enjambment here is important: the first line trumpets the abstract metaphysics of his Reality–Imagination complex, but the place-name specificity of the second line completely qualifies this. This is a bizarre jump. Usually such philosophical talk is universal, its propositions true from Boston to Bombay. But with no hesitation Stevens points to one particular place on the earth where this is more true.

The point doesn't need to be laboured in a detailed reading of the succeeding cantos: V talks of 'kin', the 'land's children' and the 'vital son', and when VI has the speakers (for it is voiced throughout by a group of people) standing 'On this present ground [. . .] / Things certain sustaining us in certainty' (CP 375), there can be little doubt that these are the 'familiar things' of the preceding cantos. That Canto VII switches to the third-person plural indicates the turn away from community which the poem will finally take, but for the moment Canto VIII merely amplifies what has come before. It describes generation as 'ten thousand tumblers tumbling down // To share the day', and there is perhaps no better gloss on this than Jorie Graham's 'Self-Portrait as the Gesture Between Them [Adam and Eve]', which describes the birth of a child thus:

> 32
> where the complex mechanism fails, where the stranger appears in the clearing,
>
> 33
> out of nowhere and uncalled for, out of nowhere to share the day.
>
> (*End of Beauty* 8)

Talk of a complex mechanism failing draws on IX also, where 'A complex of emotions falls apart', and more particularly: 'The gardener's cat is dead, the gardener gone / And last year's garden grows salacious weeds' (CP 377). One is reminded of the 'second-hand garden' of the generations in 'Extraordinary References'. Stevens is clearly registering his own break with tradition – after all, he didn't continue to live in Reading, and at that point it would have seemed that the transmission of family values to his daughter was unsuccessful (viz., L 421). Yes, he might try to make an accord with John Zeller, but Canto IX shows that he did not suppose that he did not see the difficulty of it. Another 'complex of emotions' arises, 'not / So soft, so civil'. The last canto is hardest to assess:

> The personae of summer play the characters
> Of an inhuman author, who meditates
> With the gold bugs, in blue meadows, late at night.
> He does not hear his characters talk. He sees
> Them mottled, in the moodiest costumes,
>
> Of blue and yellow, sky and sun, belted
> And knotted, sashed and seamed, half pales of red,
> Half pales of green, appropriate habit for
> The huge decorum, the manner of the time,
> Part of the mottled mood of summer's whole,

In which the characters speak because they want
To speak, the fat, the roseate characters,
Free, for a moment, from malice and sudden cry,
Complete in a completed scene, speaking
Their parts as in a youthful happiness.   (CP 378)

This is one of the most beautiful paeans to nostalgia. It expresses the great need
we have for our past – all the rich emotional lustres which never seem to be
equalled in adult life – and simultaneously says good-bye to the past since it is
'Complete in a completed scene'. 'Credences of Summer' would seem to have
been one of the last poems of *Transport to Summer* to be written. (He sent
'Credences', freshly written, out for publication on 23 July 1946 [L 530], and on
12 November 1946, he sent the proofs for *Transport to Summer* back to Knopf; in
the *Letters of Wallace Stevens* there is no reference to any other poems in the
intervening period.) The 'completion' referred to here would also seem to refer
in part to his attitude towards genealogy in the poetry. While it would not play
such a prominent role in the poetry to come, its lesson had been learnt. He
would not return to the kind of Emersonian exultation that informs even a work
as recent as 'Notes Toward a Supreme Fiction'; he would remain attentive to the
significance of lineage (viz., canto II of 'The Auroras of Autumn'); and in
general, he became more attuned to and interested in the way that communities
envision the world, rather than the way the individual does (viz., Canto V of 'An
Ordinary Evening in New Haven'). The poems of *The Rock* in the face of the
world also possess all the humility of the scion. When the connection with the
past becomes tenuous, as in the beginning of the title poem of that group, and
we believe that 'It is an illusion that we were ever alive' (CP 525), we are restored
by the story of generation in the figure of the mango tree and its fruit: 'This is the
cure / Of leaves and of the ground and of ourselves' (CP 527).

2

One of the more surprising aspects of Wallace Stevens's library is not the
French cultural reviews, the philosophy, the books on Chinese culture, or travels
though France in the eighteenth century, but the abundance of novels by
Thomas Hardy (see Moynihan). It would be much more reassuring for those
critics who talk up a particularly American literary tradition to find a similar
enthusiasm for Twain or Cooper. Hardy, with his use of dialects, his love of his
Wessex landscape and its people, his sense of the country's history, and the way
in which the English class system is an integral part of his work, is a quintes-
sentially English writer. They comprise ten of a twenty-volume set and were
probably purchased when he was relatively poor in New York in his twenties.
What was the extent of his interest in the novels? The novelist appears three

times in the index of Holly Stevens's edition of the *Letters*; all are comments to Elsie Moll: the first telling that he's been reading *The Trumpet-Major* (L 85), the second recommending to her *Under the Greenwood Tree* as 'pleasantness itself' (L 85), the third his telling her that 'If my books were unpacked I think I'd read Hardy again' (L 147). The remarks belong to the period of their courtship, suggesting that Stevens was searching out books in which they could have a common interest, rather than expressing an important direction his thought was taking at the time. Moreover, many of the markings that Stevens made in the margins of his copies show that he appreciated Hardy's philosophising on the relations between the sexes.

From the discussion of family and tradition above, it might appear that I am suggesting that Stevens turned into a conservative chauvinist in his late years, closing off imaginative possibilities in the landscape in favour of familial certainties. In what follows I open out the argument to Stevens's whole career and discuss the connections between ideas of nation and nature. Hardy provides an oblique introduction to this area. First, as a Romantic novelist, he emerged from the tradition of, among others, Wordsworth and Emerson, which was germane to Stevens. Writers like these valued above all the 'spots of time' or moments when one becomes a 'transparent eyeball' in the midst of the landscape. These exaltations, these '[e]cstatic identities / Between one's self and the weather' (CP 258), extremes of emotion that confirm us as spiritual beings who are rooted in certain locales, are exactly what led T.S. Eliot in *After Strange Gods* to reject Hardy as 'a powerful personality uncurbed by any institutional attachment or by submission to any objective beliefs' in favour of more restrained writers (54). Eliot goes on to comment:

> In consequence of his self-absorption, he makes a great deal of landscape; for landscape is a passive creature which lends itself to an author's mood. Landscape is fitted too for the purposes of an author who is interested not at all in men's minds, but only in their emotions; and perhaps only in men as vehicles for emotions. It is only, indeed, in their emotional paroxysms that most of Hardy's characters come alive. (55)

Eliot's disdain here is for exactly those moments of transcendence, of emotional exaltation in the midst of nature that are so dear to Wordsworth, Emerson and Stevens, among others. But landscape is not a 'passive creature' in these moments, rather it is an invasion of expansive reality into the scope of the poem or novel. Although *Far From the Madding Crowd* (1874) was not one of the books in Stevens's collection of Hardy, Gabriel Oak's 'spot of time' towards the beginning of that novel, ringing as it is with echoes of Emerson, is of interest in this context:

Being a man not without a frequent consciousness that there was some charm in this life he led, he stood still after looking at the sky as a useful instrument, and regarded it in an appreciative spirit, as a work of art superlatively beautiful. For a moment he seemed impressed with the speaking loneliness of the scene, or rather with the complete abstraction from all its compass of the sights and sounds of man. Human shapes, interferences, troubles, and joys were all as if they were not, and there seemed to be on the shaded hemisphere of the globe no sentient being save himself; he could fancy them all gone round to the sunny side. (13–14)

Such moments of exaltation and extended vision are central to Stevens's art. They are the flashes of validation of the life of the spirit and its realisations, and any discourse that leads away from these is suspect and erroneous. Gabriel Oak, standing looking at the sky, his mind expanding in concert with the expanses of nature and thus gaining access to a kind of touchstone of being, is undergoing a similar experience to the speaker in Section IV of 'Extracts to the Academy of Fine Ideas', which I discussed in the previous chapter.

Second, Stevens might also have been taken by the way in which Hardy's characters have an almost osmotic relationship with the country they live in. Figures that draw Hardy's approbation are those that move in closest concert with the plants, fauna and weather of the land, for instance Gabriel Oak above. Connected with this there is a sense in which characters like Oak are, without the horizon of nature behind them, somehow lacking in substantiality. Playing through them, the landscape itself becomes a character in the novel's drama. This is how their particular Englishness is expressed – not jingoistically, but with a deep, calm insistence on the relationship between them and the physical geography of the place they inhabit. It might have been for a similar reason that Stevens was such a fan of Willa Cather, as her characters' relationship with the land of Nebraska and the Southwest is very similar to Hardy's in this respect. Sending one of her novels *Sapphira and the Slave Girl* to Leonard C. van Geyzel he commented: 'Miss Cather is rather a specialty. [. . .] we have nothing better than she is' (L 381).

If we look at Stevens's 'Anecdote of Men by the Thousand' (CP 51–2) from *Harmonium*, we see this idea expressed in something like the form of a credo. The first two lines are purely philosophical, but Stevens moves swiftly to widen the poem to place, nation and identity. The Tibetan woman of this poem does not impose a style on the place she lives in, rather her land is expressed through her clothing, in similar way, it is not far fetched to add, as the landscape of Wessex speaks through a Jude Fawley or a Gabriel Oak.

That this idea remained with Stevens throughout his life is witnessed by the fact that we come across again and again in his later poetry and comments. In Canto IV of 'It Must Give Pleasure' in 'Notes Toward a Supreme Fiction' (CP 401), where we read of the 'mystic marriage in Catawba':

The great captain loved the ever-hill Catawba
And therefore married Bawda, whom he found there,
And Bawda loved the captain as she loved the sun.

They married because the marriage-place
Was what they loved.

This episode is told in the stylised manner of a fabliau (with a possible nod towards the fictional Catawba of Sinclair Lewis, who lived in Hartford in the 1920s), but nevertheless in the context of 'Notes' as a whole it is clear that Stevens respects such an osmotic relationship with the land (see also, for instance, Canto V of 'It Must Be Abstract'). Paying tribute in 1948 to John Crowe Ransom as a particularly Tennessean writer, Stevens went beyond the demands of the occasion to say what a relationship with the land of a place meant to him:

> One turns with something like ferocity toward a land that one loves, to which one is really and essentially native, to demand that it surrender, reveal, that in itself which one loves. This is a vital affair, not an affair of the heart (as it may be in one's first poems), but an affair of the whole being (as in one's last poems), a fundamental affair of life, or, rather, an affair of fundamental life; so that one's cry of O Jerusalem becomes little by little a cry to something a little nearer and nearer until at last one cries out to a living name, a living place, a living thing, and in crying out confesses openly all the bitter secretions of experience. (OP 248)

There is difficulty in recognising Ransom in Stevens's praise; it reveals more about the latter's most passionate beliefs about what poetry and life in general should be. When asked in a questionnaire in 1950 if he thought there existed 'a typical American poem', he responded: 'Even if a difference was not to be found in anything else, it could be found in what we write about. We live in two different physical worlds and it is not nonsense to think that that matters' (OP 316).

In the preceding chapter, I showed how important a consideration of nature and landscape was to his ideas of humanity in the masses and more particularly communities; how when surveying the town of New Haven Stevens moves beyond it to consider the land- and seascapes adjacent to it, as that, he believes, is how he will come to a clearer apprehension of the reality of the place, just as to know Bawda one must know Catawba; or equally, in Stevens's view, Ransom Tennessee. As I remarked in Chapter One, an important part of most nationalist movements in the nineteenth century was the artistic representation of the landscape of the nation. Thus, music like Jan Sibelius's *Finlandia* or Bedřich Smetana's *Má Vlast* was a kind of aesthetic cartography, claiming the national territory for the imagination of its people; the same kind of appropriation goes on in the poetry of, say, Whitman and Yeats, the painting of Asher Durand and Thomas Cole.

Stevens was not a chauvinist and did not extend this tradition, nevertheless he was acutely aware in this poetry how national differences both condition our apprehension of the external world and also are conditioned by that same world. For instance, a figure who encounters a new land will see it very differently from that land's indigenes. Another instance: it is a very different matter to see a picture in Russia of a dish of Russian peaches than to see the same picture in New York. This was the drift his meditation in his letter to van Geyzel on the outbreak of war and the relationship between the news and the particular place he first heard it in. In 'Imagination as Value' he discusses the way that people of different nationalities have different ideas of imaginative objects:

> The commonest idea of an imaginative object is something large. But apparently with the Japanese it is the other way round and with them the commonest idea of an imaginative object is something small. With the Hindu it appears to be something vermicular, with the Chinese, something round and with the Dutch, something square. If these evidences do not establish the point, it can hardly be because the point needs establishing. (NA 143)

But what does need establishing is the centrality of such an idea to many of Stevens's poems, as he plays variations on the indigene and the alien, making such imaginative objects collide and reconfigure themselves in the space of the poems. Nationality is a frame of vision for many speakers and figures, a frame that Stevens constantly contemplates and feints around, testing the phases of its relations with the physical geography of particular places. This is another aspect of Stevens's meditations on community and land that I discussed in the previous chapter.

The nation is a kind of enclosure that structures our perception of space. In certain respects it enhances our apprehension of the physical beauties of where we live; it does this in order to create emotional bonds that allow people to be mobilised by the State, to fight, to pay taxes, to obey laws. In other respects it suppresses or distorts of certain elements of the landscape; this is done, say, to hide patterns of ownership unfavourable to the majority of those who pay taxes, fight wars and obey laws. This inclusion/exclusion process calls to mind the well-dressed man with a beard in Chapter Two. There I showed how Stevens continually tends toward the revelation of the fecundity of interpretive possibilities when facing nature over and against those that restrict them (for instance, the other bourgeois character of the doctor of Geneva), refusing to use representations of nature in a crudely ideological way. In the context of the nation, Stevens, while respecting figures like the woman of Lhasa, knows that over generations communities create mythologies with their attendant ethics and that these can lose contact with the land. The nation is one such structure of myths and ethics, and its frame of perception can often serve to obscure our apprehension of where we live so that the land is not surrendered or revealed through it, but suppressed, distanced, erased.

These are the poles Stevens moves between: the perspicacious indigene of Lhasa or Bawda, and the view of the alien who comes to a country for the first time, knowing nothing of the ways that the indigenes view it, and able to catch something of the flauntings of first fortune I mentioned in Chapter Four. In poem after poem arguments and imagery commute back and forth between these opposites. Of course, the pole of Bawda is a kind of nostalgia – he does not seriously propose a return to such a state of things – but he acknowledges its force for the human imagination. No matter how sophisticated or cultured we become we always harbour a desire to reach back to an unmediated relation with the land; in fact the more cultured or sophisticated the more likely the desire will be stronger. As he puts it in 'Notes Toward a Supreme Fiction': 'We move between these points: / From that ever-early candor to its late plural' (CP 382). One can see these two poles present as his tribute to Ransom continues, when he says that poets must not just feel these emotions towards the land but must strive to understand them. Once they do that, 'they cease to be natives. They become outsiders. Yet it is certain that they will become insiders again. In ceasing to be native they have become insiders and outsiders at once' (OP 248). It is becoming less obvious what Stevens is driving at in relation to Ransom, but clearly in evidence are the poles of his argument as described above.

Crispin is an alien who immigrates to America with plans to found a large colony, and thus is kindred to the first American settlers. Arguably Stevens's preoccupation with the alien and immigrant is particularly American. His sense that an immigrant new to the American landscape will remake and refresh the natives' own apprehension of it connects with larger patterns of American thought. This sense of new arrivals, with their new vocabularies and new ways of describing the world, is fundamental to Stevens's thought. In 'Prologues to What Is Possible' (CP 515–17) from *The Rock*, he talks of

A flick which added to what was real and its vocabulary,
The way some first thing coming into Northern trees
Adds to them the whole vocabulary of the South,
The way the earliest single light in the evening sky, in spring,
Creates a fresh universe out of nothingness by adding itself,
The way a look or a touch reveals its unexpected magnitudes.

Throughout the last part of the *Collected Poems* there is a profound excitement at the possibilities of such change. In the very last poem of the volume, 'Not Ideas about the Thing but the Thing Itself' (CP 534), we feel that we shall walk out the door of the house of the sleeper and see a completely new landscape, a 'new reality'. He hovers on the threshold of this change in poem after poem in *The Rock*.

The best poem to start with is 'Imago' where Stevens propels all such framing structures as nations through the air and observes the results. Presumably, we can forgo the entomological meaning of the title for, with a little adjustment, the psychoanalytic one of the infantile subconscious idea of the parent or other loved one persisting in the adult. The adjustment could be as follows: 'imago' here means the subconscious idea of national community, the idea of a father- or motherland that all citizens have. This is what holds a people together, and any changes to it change the way people think of themselves and each other; 'a kind of Marshall plan of the mind', as James Longenbach calls it (289). The poem connects this idea of the nation with the perception of the landscape. The idea occurs again in the poem, 'The Irish Cliffs of Moher' (CP 501–2), where he takes the idea of 'fatherland' as far as it will go. Of the scene with the cliffs he states, 'This is not landscape', but in fact his father. In 'Imago' (CP 439) we have the idea that the nation, or our subconscious image of it, can change the way we see the world around us. And this world is decidedly not a cityscape but a landscape with rock, glacier, sun and south wind. The final image of the homeland moving through the air is like the sky-borne theatre of Canto VI 'The Auroras of Autumn'. There the theatre was engulfed by the elements, the enclosure was surpassed and we found ourselves moving through the clouds. Here the speaker wishes that the imago of the homeland – a similar kind of habitation for the community – will undergo this Dionysian moment and move through the air once again.

In the third and fourth verses, however, it would seem that the imago is purely positive. 'Medium man [. . .] feels the imagination's mercies', feels 'Something returning from a deeper quarter, / A glacier running through delirium'. Its presence 'in the mind and heart' adds to his life, it anchors 'medium man' when he begins to feel disoriented and apart. But in the fifth verse there is a subtle change of tack. That the 'imago' makes 'this heavy rock a place' would seem to be positive, but when we are told that this place 'is not of our lives composed . . .' we wonder in what direction Stevens is moving. The ellipses keep us puzzled, until the last two lines with their wistful imperative surprise us as they directly address the homeland itself. It is as if they say, 'Yes, you make "this heavy rock a place", your "gorgeous fortitude" enriches our "imagination's hymns", and yes, we feel something from a deeper quarter because of your presence, but for all that you weigh us down, you cosset us, we are too walled in.'

The last verse expresses the need to abscond from this enclosure, the need for the Dionysian moment when all we know, all we have lived by, is 'supra-mersed', if the coinage is allowed, lifted out of the ordinary and we move through the elements of nature towards a 'new reality'. With the ventriloquy of 'The Irish Cliffs of Moher' and the nation-tossing of 'Imago' we can see a Stevens who was wary of the consolations of the indigene. Settled in one place, we start to feel the heaviness of the rock and lose our imaginative forces. We lose our ability to see the landscape in its many different aspects. Interpretations are excluded, erased from our memory. In 'Imago' such forgetfulness is connected to the realm of the social through the concept of the nation. This is after all what happens to Crispin at the end in his 'nice shady home' (CP 40): he is no longer able to apprehend the interpretive possibilities that teem in the landscape, whereas before this he had room for them all. Never having left the American continent, Stevens would seem a strange advocate of this doctrine if we did not allow the idea of being settled more scope so that it includes the idea of being settled in an ideology, a religion, an aesthetic, a mythology, a science. That these should change, that they must, was his enduring dictate. They also must bring pleasure, and they must be abstract – that is, they must abstract us from what we are settled in, and allow us to apprehend the interpretive possibilities in the site of nature. Here we see the two poles I discussed earlier: there is the desire for the imago of the nation to settle the community in a particular place, in the way that the woman of Lhasa is settled, but then as the poem ends, the conflicting desire to destroy the web of such connections in favour of something more aleatory and transient, which keeps us alive to the interpretive richness in the landscape. Fundamental for Stevens then is precisely this interview between the community and the nature in which there exist the many selves and sensuous worlds he so values. 'Imago' is different from the prevailing anti-political ideology in the US of its time, in the way that it persists in searching out the relations between a people and their place. The nation is a discourse, a template for experience that would control this interpretive plenitude with the pay-off of providing the community with a pro-tective shelter from the elements, but it must be breached, reassessed, revamped for the imagination, public and individual, to stay alive.

A much earlier poem also takes for its beginning such a questioning of the landscape, and then goes on the interrogate various modes of pictorial repre-sentation (i.e., still life and landscape painting), placing these ideas against the backdrop of the nation. 'In the Clear Season of Grapes' (CP 110–11) was not collected in the first version of *Harmonium*, but was included by Stevens in the 1930 edition. It begins by considering whether the landscape has a theme or not:

> The mountains between our lands and the sea –
> This conjunction of mountains and sea and our lands –
> Have I stopped and thought of its point before?

The possessive pronoun in 'our lands' is of interest since it draws attention to a communal interpretation of the landscape not just that of an individual imagination. In fact, it is a very nationalist-sounding declaration, presuming the possession of nature and its meaning. But this of course is what the poem works to unhinge. One is reminded of 'Anecdote of Canna' in which President X is not simply an individual observer but first and foremost an integral part of the political structure of the land. Also, just as the canna abutted on the Capitol here, so too is the landscape juxtaposed against that of the house, and inside the house a still-life arrangement. Between the first and second tercets the poem moves from an exterior to interior shot, and this is also a move from landscape painting to still life. What happens next, as Stevens tries to answer his opening question, is that he reduces everything to its colour. The scene with the pears on the plate in the house between the mountains, the sky and the sea becomes 'Vermilion smeared over green, arranged for show' with a 'gross blue under rolling bronzes'. He then states that the pears ('those carefully chosen daubs') are belittled by the huge panoramas of the landscape that surround the house (which have already been reduced to their chromatic elements).

The reduction of a scene to the elements of painting brings Stevens to a new position with respect to the panoramas of nature and their meaning. The sun and moon are not just 'flashier fruits' that outdazzle the interior pears. They belittle more profoundly than that. Elsewhere Stevens states that 'We grew used so soon, too soon, to earth itself, / As an element; to the sky, as an element' (CP 328), but what is happening here is that the colliding spaces of the still life, landscape painting and finally the verbal construction of the poem itself precipitate an awareness of nature and nation as an intricate system of balancing forces and significances. By his rearrangement of the landscape through the various frames of the panorama and the still life the 'we' of the poem is able to think again about what the land means to it. The freshening of vision is not something restricted to Friedrich-esque lone gazers but is related to the life of a community of people. It is easy to imagine the opening three lines of the poem being spoken by a figure like President X.

If nations all have a particular set of perceptions, ideas of beauty, mythology and ethics, because they are connected with different physical worlds, different landscapes, then Stevens, when he wants to convey an idea of chaos, mixes up these very categories. In the second section of 'Connoisseur of Chaos' (CP 215–16), Stevens tells us that if such a mixing of nations with their respective flora is carried out in an orderly way, then a new order is established, and that new order can, after a time, be 'as pleasant as port'. One thinks also in this context of Stevens's delight in getting packages from, among other places, Leonard van Geyzel in Ceylon; it had much to do with the incongruity of the Sinhalese objects in the suburban world of Hartford (or indeed of the presence of a Marchand painting there also). But even this order, which is a kind of surreal description of the mechanism of colonial commerce, is part of the past, as indeed the genteel phrasing of the last line here intimates. In Section III, he tells us: 'At least that was the theory, when bishops' books / Resolved the world'.

In the midst of such chaos, when the consolations and clarities of the woman of Lhasa and other indigenes are far off, Stevens instinctively turns towards the physical landscape of nature in order to find turns of thought, exemplary tropes, and above all to anchor the floating consciousness to a particular locale; or, as he puts it in 'Local Objects': 'He knew that he was spirit without a foyer / And that, in this knowledge, local objects become / More precious than the most precious objects of home' (OP 137). The foyer lost here through the theorising of the bishops is that of the nation as a frame for our awareness of the world. They mixed up the categories and now sense perception floats without a mooring. With the idea of nation abandoned, landscape comes to the fore, and a new order begins to form out of that interview. The next section pits this apprehension of the landscape and weather against the discourse of philosophy, which propounds and arranges reality also. Just as Stevens reserved his approbation for the woman of 'Sunday Morning' who turns away from the theology associated with distant Palestine in favour of her immediate phenomenal world, that is, the surrounding landscape, so we might expect Stevens to side with Statement B here. But B, which abandons the objective tone of philosophy in favour of autobiographical utterance, and imbricates the observing subject in the midst of the physical world, is in some respects the voice of the complacent indigene (viz., 'All this, *of course*, will come [. . .]', my italics). As I discussed above, these are the poles of Stevens's thought that he moves between, not settling for one consolation or the other. Thus the poem posits the figure of 'the pensive man' who can mediate the issue. The great thing, the poem proposes, is to see – intransitively in the first and most important instance, and transitively in the second, perceiving an exemplary model of the human connection with place in the figure of the eagle. As enclosure for the mind and community in general, the nation, as we saw in 'Imago', has the drawback of blunting our perception of the place we inhabit, stippled as it is with interpretive possibilities. Here replacing the nation as foyer of the spirit is the idea of a nest that spans the intricacy of the Alps without reducing their herme- neutic plenitude. They remain intricate and the eagle's eye continues to observe them thus even while making his habitation there.

These issues when seen in the context of America with its colonial past become complicated by the discourse of the continent as 'virgin land', a wilderness to be tamed and civilised. The imposition of laws for living, building and seeing by the first colonists all necessitated the violent erasure of the indigenous culture. Most thought of the continent as a *tabula rasa*, a place to realise the New Jerusalem or a new form of government; even Robert Frost in this century, in 'The Gift Outright', could describe it as a land 'unstoried, artless, unenhanced' at the time of colonisation (348). Stevens was interested in the land he lived in as particularly American, but he does not think of it simply in terms of a *tabula rasa*; in his poetry he is always alive to the traces of the past to be found in the landscape, in the same way that Thoreau was to arrow heads found in Concord. The oppo- sition of civilisation vs wilderness is one of the constitutive myths of America, an opposition that is reflected also in the racial discourse of white vs black. By taking these issues as themes in his poems, Stevens is exploring some of the most important elements of American nationality.

He complicates the idea of writing on blankness, and especially in the context of the land and nature of the United States. Such colonial imposition frequently found a place in Stevens's work but was never uncritically accepted and more often ironised. Jerome McGann comments how the proper name 'Massachusetts', with its Native American etymology, gives the lie to the proprietorial gesture of

Frost's 'The Gift Outright' (*Black Riders* 173–5). In contrast, Stevens was very aware of this kind of echo when he used such names in his work, as we see from his remarks in a letter to Thomas McGreevy. When referring to the rivers Swatara and Schuylkill that appear in 'Our Stars Come from Ireland' he tells him how the first is Native American in origin and the other Dutch (L 611). The provenance of proper names with their attendant histories often plays an important role in Stevens's work.

In the great early fable of the emigrating imagination, 'The Comedian as the Letter C', Crispin's Kantian struggles are to the fore, but more subtly, as we can see from such a title as 'The Idea of a Colony', this allegedly esoteric drama was already brushing shoulders with a different, national one. My aim in the following readings is to emphasise the connection the poetry makes between metaphysical and national levels, as Stevens faces the plenitude of interpretive possibilities in nature and plays these off against the framing structure of the nation. Landscape and nature then become the best way to explore Stevens's thoughts on nation and the way that it informs the perceiving imagination. It also becomes a way to explore further Stevens's ideas of race, and more particularly his treatment of African American figures in the poetry, which I shall look at towards the end of this chapter.

The necessity for every nation is to forge a connection between the actual land – the clay, the flora of the tract – with the discourse of the nation. In the current terminology, one must write on the land (as one supposedly does on what is called 'the body'). 'Ploughing on Sunday' (CP 20) is a hale-hearted, jocular take on this idea. It opens with curt descriptions of flora and fauna and then proclaims: 'Remus, blow your horn! / I'm ploughing on Sunday, / Ploughing North America.' The last six lines of the poem are a reprise with minimal variation on the first eight, so the pattern of the poem is: landscape–proclamation–landscape. By ploughing the continent the speaker is, by implication, putting it into shape, civilising it; Remus could be both Uncle Remus and Romulus' brother. The latter possibility implies the speaker himself is a type Romulus, more whimsical than the original but for all that the founder of a civilisation, this time in North America, writing directly on the land with his cultivating plough. That he is doing this on Sunday also indicates his abandonment of the Christian church, which had its centre for so long in Rome. In any case, the tone of the poem warns us not to take this nationalist appropriation of the continent too seriously. Stevens is much more comfortable with situations and figures that upset such alignments, as for instance in 'Our Stars Come from Ireland'.

The speaker of that poem (CP 454–5) has been abstracted from his homeland and we overhear him in the poem as he tries to interpret the landscape of the New World. The speaker of the poem is Thomas McGreevy and he looks back to Tom McGreevy-as-a-boy, who has now become another self with the passage of time and with emigration. The boy dies in Mal Bay, and the older McGreevy now lives an ocean away from his birthplace. He thinks of the boy he was and how

Mal Bay and that boy were coevals, and how when McGreevy left the place, he left a self there also. ('I am what is around me', Stevens says all the way back in *Harmonium* [cp 86].) In Mal Bay, the boy first discovered water, the stars on the water, and the music that the wind makes over the land. These all came together as a conglomerate entity that could be called 'Mal Bay and the Boy'. The tricks that Stevens plays with the tense-order brings out the ambiguity that McGreevy experiences hearing the wind now in Pennsylvania, and the fact that he first discovered its music in Tarbert. It was a sensory bundle of wind-music and place that cannot be untied without consequence. The consequence of the migration, as the third verse tells us, is death, or at least the death of a self. In the fourth verse, the complexity increases: first he repeats that it is from this dead boy that Mal Bay came, not from the *Weltanschauung* of a 'bald and tasselled saint'. McGreevy then asks: 'What would the water have been, / Without that that he makes of it?' The present tense of the verb 'make' upsets things completely. The boy is dead, but still this tense is predicated of him. What is a dead self that it is still making? Part of this boy is in Pennsylvania making things out of water now, out of the rivers of Schuylkill and Swatara. This two-line, exasperatingly ambiguous question precipitates others. What is water, in Pennsylvania or Tarbert? How much is the boy still alive with his own particular synaesthesias, now in Pennsylvania? How can an immigrant, a 'beautiful and abandoned' refugee, see the land, even the simplest things like the reflection stars make on a river? The speaker is confused as he tries to interpret his new surroundings. There is a competition of names in the poem also, from three languages, Irish, Dutch and Iroquoian, whose place names have been transliterated into English.

Mal Bay	Tarbert	Kerry
Swatara	Schuylkill	

They compete in the syntactical miasma of the poem to name the be-starred water, reminding us of the etymological trickery of 'The Countryman' where the river Swatara is 'a swarthy presence moving, / Slowly, to the look of a swarthy name' (cp 429). Although Swatara – a black river we are told – has an Iroquoian etymology that means 'place of eels', Stevens yokes it with the word swarthy, meaning black in German. Stevens tells us that 'Being there is being in a place, / As of a character everywhere', and yet this character of the place is a complex thing if its proper names are anything to go by. Stevens, through his play on these etymons, registers the traces of history – personal and national – in the landscape. He also shows the complexity involved in our perception of the land when the frames of nation are rearranged, here by the journey of an immigrant.

For Tom McGreevy, as an immigrant, imagined by Stevens for this poem, saying what the water of the United States actually is, is not such an easy thing either. His mind is the post-colonial imagination in small. However, if we consider the last line on its own, everything is resolved: 'The ocean breathed out

morning in one breath.' The ocean ex-presses the sun, pushes it out unambig-
uously. This breathing also conjures the physical aspect of the act of naming
something: breath is expelled as you make the sound 'Schuylkill' or 'Tarbert'. But
of course there is no such resolution. It is restrained by the first line of the last
verse, with the two words 'as if'. In 'The Countryman', it was the ironic contami-
nation of the German etymology of the word 'swarthy' that cast doubts on the
naming that went on in the poem, and here the resolution of the ocean's one
breath is held back because the land, for Tom McGreevy, is still ambiguous. This
ocean-breath could be thought of as a kind of an autochthonous American
mythopoeia, only the possibility of which, at this stage, can be entertained, not
asserted. But nevertheless, he still places this line at the end, thus giving the poem
an impression of formal closure.

What such a poem as this conveys is the problematic of the land and nature
of the United States as an individual awareness finds and interprets it. We are
drawn through the confusions of the immigrant who cannot give a coherent
interpretation to what he perceives of the rivers, mountains, stars, and skies,
which he finds in Pennsylvania. It shows him erratically maintained by redundant
proper names, sense-impressions of cypher-like stars on the water, and a syntax
that lets meaning constantly glissade off into polyvalence. McGreevy is, by
synecdoche, every other Irish immigrant, and widening the scope further, every
immigrant that arrived on the continent from Europe over the last few hundred
years. This poem goes down to the foundations of our ideas of nation – direct
human perception – and attempts to interpret the New World through them.

In 'Our Stars' the dislocations experienced by the alien in the new land do not
threaten disintegration of the McGreevy figure: the meditative tone conveys the
knowledge that these matters will be finally resolved; or, if they are not it is possible
to live with them. The speaker of 'A Dish of Peaches in Russia' (CP 224) feels no
such comfort. He is an exiled Russian looking at a painting of a dish of peaches
in his native town in Russia. He absorbs them, he tells us, 'as the Angevine /
Absorbs Anjou', or, we might add, as the Lhasan woman Lhasa. He inhales their
aura and exalts: 'Ah! and red; and they have peach fuzz, ah!' But although the
painting brings him back to his homeland in his imagination, he is physically
standing elsewhere. The movement of the curtains in the gallery where the
Russian exile is looking at the painting, however gentle, is what brings him back
to his true location. The poem achieves dramatic effect through the contrast of
that movement with the 'ferocities' that invade the poem in the last distich. What
the poem insists on is the forceful impact of such dislocations of nation on the very
act of perception. The peaches, as objects taken from nature, stand as synecdoche
for the landscape the Russian knows and loves – they are taken from it and
placed in the painting, which is then transported to America, in the same way as
the flowers were in 'The Bouquet'.

In 'An Ordinary Evening in New Haven' Stevens opens a canto with:
'Inescapable romance, inescapable choice / Of dreams' (CP 468), and goes on

to refer to 'A great town hanging pendent in a shade, / An enormous nation happy in a style'. It is this kind of indigenous arrangement that the arrival of the immigrant disturbs. The indigene has become so immersed in his homeland that he longer experiences hermeneutic uncertainty when looking at the landscape: it is transparently clear to him. The gaze of the indigene thus erases all interpretive differences. The immigrant, however, has a different vocabulary, a different myth to explain the moon and sun, river and mountain, and as a result he augurs a new reality. The town is enclosed within the shade, the nation enclosed within the style. Nothing will change until there is difference. As he said of such happiness in 'The Auroras of Autumn' (CP 420):

> A happy people in an unhappy world –
> It cannot be. There's nothing there to roll
>
> On the expressive tongue, the finding fang.
> A happy people in a happy world –
> Buffo! A ball, an opera, a bar.

He settles for an 'unhappy people in a happy world', which is a good description of immigrants. These are the 'secretive syllables' that he solemnises. Such an imbalance of happiness fosters awareness, fosters the interpreting imagination. The immigrant observes his surroundings with more urgency than the indigene as he tries to square the new world with the old world he grew up in. As we saw in 'Our Stars' Stevens follows these inquiries as the immigrant faces the landscape.

Although 'Our Stars' and 'An Ordinary Evening in New Haven' are both poems from the late collection, *The Auroras of Autumn* (1950), there is a consistency of theme in Stevens's oeuvre that allows us to look back to his first collection and see the same idea. ('Two at Norfolk' did not appear in the 1923 edition of *Harmonium*, but was added in 1930.) For instance, there is 'The Doctor of Geneva', 'The Cuban Doctor' and 'Herr Doktor' of 'Delightful Evening'. All three have their doctrines of the landscape but find themselves in foreign parts with strange results. More accustomed to European lakes than huge oceans, the first waxes petulant when facing the Pacific swell: 'Lacustrine man had never been assailed / By such long-rolling opulent cataracts' (CP 24). 'He did not quail', we are told and yet the ocean found means 'to set his simmering mind / Spinning and hissing with oracular / Notations of the wild'. And no matter where the Cuban doctor goes he cannot escape his enemy, the Indian. He cannot clean the sky of his image (CP 64).

The phases of this difference between immigrants and their adopted worlds are sung in comic major keys as well as these somewhat mournful minor ones. The macabre mice do not perhaps have resident alien status in the land of the turkeys and that makes their dance all the more mischievous (CP 123). Stevens rises to a rhyming couplet for comic effect in the first verse where we see the immigrant rodents making free with a solemn turkey monument.

In the land of the turkeys in turkey weather
At the base of the statue, we go round and round.
What a beautiful history, beautiful surprise!
Monsieur is on horseback. The horse is covered with mice.

Benjamin Franklin suggested, perhaps not altogether seriously, that the turkey could serve as a national symbol for the United States, and this twelve-liner is perhaps quipping at the expense of those States. And although this comic piece is not worked out in terms of landscape and nature, its message is clear: it is impossible to stop the influx of immigrants with their revisionary vocabularies that break down the 'lordly language of the inscription' on the historical monument. Dismissively they refer to 'The Founder of the State', and ask, 'Whoever founded / A state that was free, in the dead of winter, from mice?'

In 'The Pure Good of Theory' (CP 329–33) we are told how the landscape of Brazil nourished 'the emaciated / Romantic with dreams of her avoirdupois'. The lushness of the natural world in this poem combined with ideas of the romantic has created a 'new reality' and it is no bad description of romanticisation of the continent of the New World. We think of painters like Asher Durand, poets like Bryant and Whittier. Werther is revived with smelling salts and transported to Rio. The flag of the turkeys is replaced by the 'flag of the nude' – nudity, for Stevens, implying an immediacy of sensation and fecundity of imagination. It is also associated with a willingness to brave the elements, to leave all protecting shelters – the coat, the house, the capitol – and walk out under the sky to see what the weather holds in store for humanity. But here this nakedness is merely a token: although the flag proudly flies, no one braves the elements in his or her pelt. The romantic 'new reality' is quite decadent at this stage and it takes a new immigrant to renovate the landscape and natural world. It turns out that 'He was a Jew from Europe or might have been'. As before, it is the immigrant who sees from the outside a nation happy in its style. He is the angel of reality, the 'heavenly foreigner', to use Denis Devlin's phrase, upon whom the future depends. It is only such a figure that can 'stick to the nicer knowledge of / Belief, that what it believes in is not true' (CP 332). All this takes place in the scene with the green glade, the rivers simmering by, the hotel and sea stretching out from the land of Brazil. As in 'Our Stars', the immigrant is immersed in the landscape and must interpret it.

Another form that this idea – the nation as an enclosure that must be breached – takes is the recurring notion that the weather, the sun, stars and moon of America come from other countries. Although they inhabit an American sky, they are not American and our whole view of the American landscape is transformed by this realisation. As witnessed by his letters to acquaintances and friends in every part of the world, from Paris to Ceylon, Stevens had a great imaginative need for the idea of *elsewhere*.[2] Receiving gifts from China that were not normally available in the United States thrilled him. They helped set off the mundane world of Hartford. As his imagination dwelled on these distant places, he became an honorary immigrant himself, gaining access to the immigrant's renovating vision. This gave him an imaginative power to clear the world of its 'stiff and stubborn, man-locked set'. It let him see Asian tigers creeping across the sky (CP 153). Even workaday Hartford cannot withstand this power (CP 226):

> A long time you have been making the trip
> From Havre to Hartford, Master Soleil,
> Bringing the lights of Norway and all that.

But sometimes for those figures of incapable imagination, such breaches of the national borders can be dangerous. As maleficent winds whirl upon one 'weak-minded' speaker of a poem, he ends up falling, the blood of his mind seeping across the floor (CP 212). The fight he has lost is recounted in the preceding stanza.

>   at night,
> The wind of Iceland and
> The wind of Ceylon,
> Meeting, gripped my mind,
> Gripped it and grappled my thoughts.

Finally, he can only dream of a figure who 'Could have touched these winds, / Bent and broken them down'.

The dynamic of pastoral and political is at work in 'Dutch Graves in Bucks County' (CP 290–3), where Stevens verges on the allegorical as he places representations of the machines of war into the sky above Pennsylvania. Those machines were at work in the European theatre but it is indicative of the strength of the pattern of thought that I have described above that Stevens needs to see them in the pastoral context in order to get at their meaning fully and gauge them against the land and traditions of the US. The poem is addressed to the ghosts of the first Dutch settlers whose repose contrasts with the activity of the angry men of the present and their furious machines. Stevens's own ancestors on his father's side lived in Bucks County and in this way, quietly but insistently, the poem strikes the note of the personal, as did Section IV of 'Credences'. They were once immigrants, but through the generations mixed themselves with the land so that they have an indigenous presence in the land. But in the present of the poem, they find themselves in a strange land again just as they first did centuries ago. They are alienated by the mindless and hubristic warring parties of the present whose anthem is the 'hullabaloo of health and have'. Their chaos, the chaos of their arcs of organisation, is ardour more than order. Theirs is a 'storm of torn-up testaments', a forgetfulness, a deafness to what and who preceded them. They swarm over the old temples and, observing this, Stevens addresses the Dutch ghosts thus:

> Time was not wasted in your subtle temples.
> No: nor divergence made too steep to follow down.

This can be read in two ways: 'You did not waste your time building and worshipping in your temples'; or: 'They didn't stay, these men of the present, for a moment to consider what you had done'. The second meaning undercuts the consolation of the first. Stevens does not fully condemn the present, moreover he does not refrain from showing his ancestors in a slightly comical light, as they 'tap skeleton drums inaudibly'. He sees a necessity in the present glory, but also its end. For all their airborne anger, Stevens's prolepsis has them sliding down into the ground. This poem has skies and graves, autumn horizons and dark compartments in the earth. In addition, the poem has a grand historical sweep – from the first Dutch settlers to the violent, technological present – and it is an oblique attempt to think about the course of US history: the land settled long ago by immigrants and now involved in a fiercely modern war in Europe. Alan Filreis points out that the Dutch graves of the poem are a reminder of America's responsibilities in the European conflict (*Actual World* 119). In their moment of achievement they are dismissive of their forefathers who lie under them in the earth: Stevens lets their rhetoric into the poem, as they ask: 'Who are the mossy cronies muttering, / Monsters antique and haggard with past thought?' As is witnessed by the sums of money that he devoted to finding them, Stevens was not quite as dismissive of his Dutch forbears (viz., his many letters to Lila James Roney, mainly from 1942 to 1947, whom Stevens hired to research his ancestry). The poem is also important for the way in which it is pivoted between his earlier preoccupation with confronting the great masses of men and his later meditations on community, place and tradition. Both poles are pitted against each other here.

The dead immigrants are literally immersed in the landscape, and it is to landscape that we return to after the ambitious generation has failed. 'No Possum, No Sop, No Taters' (CP 293–4) shows the morning after anger, aspiration and war.

> He is not here, the old sun,
> As absent as if we were asleep.
>
> The field is frozen. The leaves are dry.

The rhetorical energy of 'Dutch Graves' is absent also. The sentences are clipped, minimalist like bleak early Mondrian landscapes. In the previous poem Stevens had the phases of the difference between the dead immigrants and the new generation to sing, but here all such differences have collapsed, leaving us with desolation.

Whereas 'Dutch Graves' was exhilarated by blood and mutilation ('Freedom is like a man who kills himself / Each night, an incessant butcher, whose knife / Grows sharp in blood.'), in 'No Possum', we see the bleak mess that this leaves: 'the broken stalks / Have arms without hands. They have trunks // Without legs or, for that, without heads.' The desolate landscape of the field and tree (with its malicious crow) is the scene to which the imagination must return in order to start its projects once more ('It is here, in this bad, that we reach / The last purity of the knowledge of good'), and not some Cartesian 'extension', or the blankness of 'reality', but a landscape, the fundamental arena of consciousness for Stevens.

He turns to praise the indigene in 'Lebensweisheitspielerei'. It is not a moment of rich indulgence or imaginative celebration of the type that might be associated with the wedding of Bawda and her captain. It is a moment of reduced power, when being a native in a place does not entail a distortion of reality, but rather enables a clearer vision of that reality, much in the way that the propositions chalked on the pavement in 'Connoisseur of Chaos' enabled the pensive man to see better. This moment of reconciliation with the view of the indigene is typical of the last stage of Stevens's career. The poems of The Rock are closest in their metaphysical approximations to actual places: the suburban locales in which Stevens spent his life are clearly visible, yet so are the magisterial abstractions that animate his thought. It is a kind of grand détente. The title of the poem in English means 'worldly wisdom's game' but it is written in German as 'Lebensweisheitspielerei' (CP 504–5). This choice of a German title is worth noting in a poem about natives. It perhaps alludes to the grand metaphysical systems of philosophers like Kant, Hegel and Schopenhauer, reminding us of the line in 'The Plain Sense of Things': 'The great structure has become a minor house'. Stevens puns on the words 'indigence' and 'indigene', etymological *faux amis*. Here the arrival of an alien would not help the natives of this place towards clearer vision as they are already stripped of all illusions about their place in the world. This is the kind of habitation that Stevens favours over the enclosure of the nation: the community of the poem are drawn together and are 'Natives of a dwindled sphere', but natives nonetheless and living within a shared reality that allows them to perceive one another most clearly: 'Each person completely touches us / With what he is and as he is'; and this 'touching' can be both physical and emotional. There is no 'national load' like that referred to in 'Imago' and this gives access to feelings and awarenesses long suppressed.

These are instances of a feature of Stevens's poetry that I have been driving at in this book: his tendency to draw all issues into the arena of immediate perception and to make them play out their significance there. As I showed in Chapter One, to get at the essence of Marxism he seats Lenin on a suburban park bench and observes what transformations his ideology carries out on the surrounding space. Similarly to think about the nation here he examines the skies over Hartford for other national influences. If one lives in America, what are we to make of a French-looking sun? At other points when he thinks of social change or ultimate politicians he pictures a building in a ruinous storm, allowing abstractions to take on body in space so that they can be perceived, walked around, considered and accepted or abandoned. His is a particularly plastic imagination in this respect. This is the politico-pastoral space of the poems. Stevens is attracted to the atmospheres and locales of traditional pastoral poetry, but also lets wider social and political concerns play through this space.

But, given this, what are we to make of the directive that civilisation must be in touch with the land, must in some way be 'blooded' by it? How desirable is it for the institutions of a nation to be in contact with the land? After all, that very contact was what the Fascist movements of the twentieth century so proudly bruited and put to terrible ends. But what Stevens gives us in the poems is not a set of rules for the healthy running of nation states: nature is not presented as some inviolable good that must be ingested by political structures and subsequently deployed to bolster their ideologies. Rather, Stevens interrogates and tests those structures in the space of nature to see how well they react to contingency, flux, uncertainty. Konstantinov clearly fails, the ideology holding together the people of 'The Common Life' also. It might be felt that this is not political poetry at all and that it is inaccurate to talk of such a politico-pastoral space in the poems; there is pastoral, yes, but very little of what is commonly meant by the word politics, which involves choice, action, specific allegiances.

As I argued in Chapter Three, there is a place for a poetry of politics that is not so engaged, a poetry that is kind of space for public dreaming and is lifted free of immediate civic responsibilities yet which lets us reimagine or reconfirm those choices, actions and allegiances. What Stevens gives us are images of ourselves in communities, fostering the awareness of the historical course of those communities. The hard work of course begins when the book of poetry is put down and lasting public institutions and laws must be built and maintained. Poetry and art in general will never really help when making those decisions but for the vision it gives of the wider horizon of such public choice it is invaluable. It will not always do this and there will be always be counter-examples (a favourite is the concentration camp commandant listening to Mozart), and yet that poetry is capable of doing this on occasion is enough.

3

Earlier I drew attention to the poles of indigene and alien and related this to the idea of nation in Stevens's poetry. I proposed that such issues become interestingly complex in the context of America and its colonial history. As I also remarked, the opposition of wilderness-civilisation is replicated in his thinking about race with African-American figures standing in as symbols of primitiveness, savagery, closeness to the land, in contrast to the white civilisation that is divorced from nature and must constantly be brought back to an awareness of it. Anthony

Hecht has referred to Stevens's 'incorrigible racism' (38), and in a perceptive essay, Lisa DuRose points out that while Stevens often makes statements of solidarity with African Americans, he never moves beyond stereotypical representation of them in the poetry. She asks what the value of the manoeuvre is and finds that his adoption of blackface allows him to criticise various elements of bourgeois white culture; the 'nigger' motif serves only as a foil and Stevens remains uninterested in exploring the complexities of racial representation as he did the relationship between nation and landscape.

In a poem like 'Two at Norfolk' (CP 111–12) we can see a kind of apartheid of the imagination at work, implying that the free play of the imagination in the landscape, the facing of all those interpretive possibilities, is restricted to the free play of *white* imagination. It opens with the order: 'Mow the grass in the cemetery, darkies', implying that however much he might have welcomed new realities Stevens did not envisage them coming from certain quarters. Although the poem is about immigration it is interesting that he does not stop to consider how these 'darkies' came to be mowing grass in Connecticut. It makes no sense to think of this kind of racism as the same as the anti-Semitism of Eliot and Pound, nevertheless Stevens's command here, and his use of coloured stereotypes elsewhere in the poetry, is disconcerting.

The delight in the provisionality and abundance of interpretations of nature and landscape in Stevens's poetry begins to appear culpable. One could argue that the use of coloured stereotypes is incidental to an art that constantly theorises the inclusion–exclusion dialectic and that Stevens's poetry can be co-opted by those seeking to change an objectionable status quo. But the problem with this is that Stevens's use of words like 'Sambo', 'darkies' and 'nigger' relays a clear message to the African-American reader that he or she is not expected to partake in the '[e]cstatic identities / Between one's self and the weather', in the same complex way as, say, the pensive man does at the end of 'Connoisseur of Chaos'. In other instances Stevens's poetry *is* available to the marginalised because the point it makes, especially in a poem like 'On the Road Home', is that monolithic truths and totalising worldviews are arbitrary and unstable. This is witnessed by the way in which Adrienne Rich, a very different poet indeed, found that Stevens's work was important to her at a crucial juncture in her career (197–205). As a white reader of Stevens's poetry it is dismaying to think that he blithely disallows so many from taking pleasure in his work on the basis of race. Of course he is not vitriolic: he simply employs certain racial stereotypes without asking us to hate them. But such casual racism is nevertheless distasteful.

If there is a drawback, however, to the kind of reading of DuRose's it is that it is monochrome. Far from being a discussion of race in Stevens it is concerned only with his treatment of African Americans, passing over his representations of Chinese, Polish, Irish, Native American, and Dutch, among others in the poems. Stevens's racial mosaic is more complex and there are other figures of other races who do not move beyond stereotype. There is no doubt that DuRose's central argument that Stevens's representations of African Americans are restricted by prejudice is correct, but worth considering in this context is how his representations of many other groups was similarly limited. Mark Halliday in his *Wallace Stevens and the Interpersonal* shows how his treatment of the poor and suffering is distant, how his portrayals of women are similarly lacking, but also he shows that there is a very special compensation for these omissions in the relationship he creates with the reader. In his fourth chapter, Halliday traces out the richness and complexity of this relationship arguing that Stevens empowers the reader, makes him feel involved and important in the unfolding debates and dramatic situations of the poems. One reply to this from one of the slighted groups might be that it is obvious from the images of the poor and suffering, of women, of African Americans, that Stevens never meant for such a rich and complex relationship between writer and reader to be with *them*. Maybe he didn't, but if this is the only basis for dismissing Stevens on the grounds of race then it is flimsy, and one that restricts the appreciation and production of literature.

What I mean can be best explained not by going further into the debates about identity politics in the US, but by looking at an analogous situation, that of Ireland and England. For centuries the Irish held a position in English minds somewhat similar to Blacks for Americans. Even the meaning of the word Irish still means 'stupid' in England today, or as the *OED* tactfully puts it, 'having what are considered Irish characteristics'. In the literary context, many writers shared these prejudices. But now witness how Irish writers of this century have learnt from their English predecessors. This is not subservience to the English tradition, rather they use it for their own ends. Recognition like this is not just homage but enables subversion also. The important point is that they recognise their important forbears and in the process make us read them again with their transformations in mind. In this way Stevens can be read against himself, as it were, by African-American writers and critics; blanket dismissal merely repeats the error of Stevens and other writers like him in their treatment of race.

But there is a brief flashing moment when all these issues are turned on their head. It is one of those Imagist vignettes that Stevens was so fond of in his early career. The poem appeared in the first edition of *Harmonium* but was removed from the second. It transfers the idea of skin-colour with all its attendant social significance into the realm of aesthetic apprehension of reality as merely a succession of colours and forms. The move is typical of the turn toward abstraction that is to be found not just in Stevens's poetry during this period but in the poetry and art of the era, both in America and Europe. When seen in this context of race and aliens and indigenes 'The Silver Plough-Boy' (OP 17) takes on a poignant, lyrical aspect, which is admittedly somewhat overdone in the poem's final line. But its central image glitters before us suggesting the overturning of the savage–civilised opposition within which Stevens elsewhere viewed African Americans, suggesting that there are zones of perception into which both white and non-white pass, and perform there a strange arabesque that confuses entrenched social categories. It also turns on its head the whole idea of the Caucasian as the blank canvass, which is then contaminated by other colours. Here blackness is the base, and the lighter shades adopted. The plough-boy passes from one colour to the other, and night fades into day; in the hushed aura of aesthetic appreciation that poem creates, social characteristics are not erased but confounded, just as in 'Imago' where Stevens valued the moment when the national categories are airborne, moving from one state to the next. Toni Morrison in *Playing in the Dark*, the text that DuRose uses to map out her considerations of race in Stevens, reads racial patterns in Edgar Allan Poe's treatment of blackness and whiteness even when dissociated from skin colour (32–3); here, then, in 'The Silver Plough-Boy' is a racial ideology that fits much better with Stevens's more general thoughts about ideas of order culture and society, one in which there are glittering passages from one category to the next, in the constant creation of new orders of race and nation.

In this book I have argued that there is a special politico-pastoral space in Stevens's poetry that sets the parameters for his thinking on human groupings, be they nations, communities, or great masses of men. His thoughts about ideology are informed at every turn by the natural world, as though he wanted to make ideology *answerable* to the metamorphoses sweeping through the sky and the landscape extending around. Stuart M. Sperry remarked how '[t]he concept of *weather* is immensely important to Stevens [. . .] because it indicates the point at which the essential conditions of our environment meet and merge with our subjective sensibilities, which react to and interpret them [. . .]' (606). Stevens's poetry makes ideology and politics *physical* so that it takes on body with that arena of subjective sensibility, as for instance I showed in 'Dutch Graves'. The fundamental tenet of such an approach to space, as I indicated at the outset, is that if ideological and societal matters have any reality then they should affect the very scene before our eyes, even if that is an atmosphere as rarefied as a bouquet standing on a table in an empty house. If one's antennae are adequately sensitive then the barricades, the bombs, the transformation from monarchy to Marxism, all should be observable in the shapes of the petals, the position of the vase, the very texture of air in the room.

I have shown how many poems turn between these considerations, in the way that Shakespearean sonnets turn in the final couplet. Perhaps this is, as Rob Wilson intimates, the last great nature poetry for us, and that the natural as category has got lost in the postmodern sublime (206). Perhaps Stevens's auroras, rocks and flaming Floridian fronds merely cater to our nostalgia. However, what remains of importance is Stevens's figurations of the political imagination, his attempt to envisage communities, their desires, mythologies, polities. This is for me political poetry in the best and deepest sense, one that speaks intimately with its reader without forgoing wider public panoramas. For Stevens the pastoral tradition served this purpose; for more recent poets there are different means. Attending to their words, we attend to the political and cultural world around us, its deep configurations that pattern the air we breathe, the space we see, the skies we live beneath.

Notes

Introduction

1   I am thinking here of the emergence of the Association of Literary Scholars and Critics in opposition to the Modern Language Association, and, among other books, Harold Bloom's *The Western Canon: The Books and the School of the Ages* (1994). Also, Helen Vendler, perhaps the best reader of poetry on both sides of the Atlantic, in the introduction to *The Art of Shakespeare's Sonnets* (1997), comments: 'I do not regard as literary criticism any set of remarks about a poem which would be equally true of its paraphrasable propositional content' (xiii).

Chapter 1

1   Andrew Zawacki pointed out to me that Emerson is not quite as disengaged from politics as I would have him here, referring me to the following passage from 'Nature': 'The critics who complain of the sickly separation of the beauty of nature from the thing to be done, must consider that our hunting of the picturesque is inseparable from our protest against false society' (395). This quotation makes Emerson look like the Stevens of my argument here. However, Emerson was never really capable of making this connection between the exaltations experienced by viewers of the picturesque and the organisation of society; in much of his work he is simply not concerned with such a project. Emerson's failure to think in terms of ideology when mapping out Transcendentalism is discussed by John Carlos Rowe in the first two chapters of *At Emerson's Tomb: The Politics of Classic American Literature* (1997).

Chapter 2

1   Shortly after declaring that Nature is not in fact what we commonly think of as hills, trees, lakes, in short, a landscape untouched by humanity, Emerson asserts the necessity of going into solitude in order to experience the moments of transcendental awareness, which are the cornerstones of his philosophical outlook. 'To go into solitude, a man needs to retire as much from his chamber as from society' (5). In other words, a man must go into what is commonly thought of as Nature. It is on the site of this solitude in natural wilderness that all the insights that follow occur.

2   Jeffers tried to mitigate this attitude once in an introduction to a collection by describing his 'Inhumanism' thus: '[. . .] a certain philosophical attitude, which might be

called Inhumanism, a shifting of emphasis and significance from man to not-man [. . .] This manner of thought and feeling is neither misanthropic nor pessimist; [. . .] it has objective truth and human value. It offers a reasonable detachment as rule of conduct, instead of love, hate and envy. It neutralizes fanaticism and wild hopes; but it provides magnificence for the religious instinct, and satisfies our need to admire greatness and rejoice in beauty' (qtd by Carpenter 127). But such statements ring hollow in the face of the poetry.

3   Alan Perlis observes that 'Stevens devastates Ludwig Richter with a whimsical exercise in imaginative vision' (37); Daniel T O'Hara says of the poem that '[t]he entire theatre of the world, facing its apocalypse, has become a poor man's version of Wagner produced by a grandiloquent fool' (37); and Helen Vendler, in *Words Chosen Out of Desire*, writes that the poem 'treats its own problem with indifferent irony. The hero is "Ludwig Richter, turbulent Schlemihl," and his sufferings are watched through a monocle' (13). For an engaging reading of this poem see Chris Beyers's article, 'Stevens and Ludwig Richter', where Beyers surmises on the possible sources of Stevens's Richter, plunking, with an educated guess, for Ruskin. However what Beyers does not mention in his article is that Stevens read German and could well have received the book from Europe.

4   Bonnie Costello places a different emphasis on Stevens's relation to the visual arts, suggesting that painting represented 'a path to immanence not available in poetry (at least in the highly discursive and rhetorical poetry of Wallace Stevens)' ('Effects of an Analogy' 70). But Stevens was not consistent in such matters, and so it is no surprise that Richter's art plays a very different role to that which Costello describes. In 'Chaos in Motion', Richter is chosen precisely because his work does not suggest a path to immanence, and it is by figuring that painter's disintegration that Stevens affords us a glimpse of the natural object that Richter's representation occluded. However Costello is right when she observes in her reading of 'Add This to Rhetoric', that finally Stevens remains ambivalent about all representation, whether verbal or figural (71). My reading of 'Chaos in Motion', in this context, confirms Costello's point.

5   When excerpting from the poem for the a selection of his work submitted to Knopf in 1950 (but which remained unpublished), he made sure Section XIII was there too preceding the final section (ms. in the Huntington Collection).

6   Once again as in 'Dry Loaf' and 'The Well Dressed Man', Stevens criticises the figure who uses landscape and weather to abscond from society: 'Men and the affairs of men seldom concerned / This pundit of the weather, who never ceased / To think of man the abstraction, the comic sum' (XXXV).

Chapter 3

1   John Barrell puts it thus: 'I shall argue that this [social] vision of rural life [in England] can be understood only by understanding the constraints—often apparently aesthetic but in fact moral and social—that determined how the poor could, or rather how they could *not* be represented; and that we can understand these constraints by attempting to understand the imagery of the paintings I discuss, and how it relates to their organisation as

pictures' (2). Also of interest here is Chris Fitter's *Poetry, Space, Landscape* (1995), which investigates the social and ideological contexts of landscape representation in poetry, concluding with readings of seventeenth-century English poetry.

Chapter 4

1   As he says in 'The Relations between Poetry and Painting':

> Under such stress, reality changes from substance to sublety [*sic*], a sublety [*sic*] in which it was natural for Cézanne to say: 'I see planes bestriding each other and sometimes straight lines seem to me to fall' or 'Planes in color. . . . The colored area where shimmer the souls of the planes, in the blaze of the kindled prism, the meeting of planes in the sunlight.' (NA 174)

And he continues, citing Paul Klee, to show just how much of a shift in sensibility and culture is behind this reduction to colour and shape: it is nothing less than the creation of 'a new reality, a modern reality'.

2   This might refer us to Canto VI where the use of the word 'vassal' is striking in a poem by a US poet. Its origins are in feudal Europe. Alpha, in comparison with Omega 'Of dense investiture, with luminous vassals [. . .]', is naked. Naked, like an indigenous American, is perhaps too much to suggest, but nevertheless Stevens could be using the image of nakedness to suggest a more immediate relationship with nature, as he does elsewhere.

Chapter 5

1   Here I pass over Thomas Lombardi's *Wallace Stevens and the Pennsylvania Keystone* (1996) which is concerned with relating Stevens's poetry to the part of Pennsylvania he was raised in. While the book is useful as a resource of biographical data, with dogged consistency, it tendentiously employs this data in its readings of the poetry so that even the landscapes of Florida, where Stevens occasionally holidayed, fade to reveal Pennsylvania.

2   See, for instance, his letters to Leonard van Geyzel, such as (L 327), and the following: 'Your letter came as a surprise: a welcome one. It has always made Ceylon seem more reasonable to know someone like oneself out there, in the same way that the existence of a St Michael's Church in Colombo makes the place interchangeable with Toronto or some other place equally recognizable' (L 838). Also his numerous letters to the Vidals, José Rodríguez Feo and Peter Lee bear witness to this fact. The idea is perhaps clearest in his correspondence with Feo collected in *Secretaries of the Moon: The Letters of Wallace Stevens and José Rodríguez Feo*.

Works cited

Abraham, Gerald, ed. *New Oxford History of Music: The Age of Beethoven 1790–1830*. Vol. 8. Oxford: Oxford UP, 1982.

Altieri, Charles. *Canons and Consequences: Reflections on the Ethical Force of Imaginative Ideals*. Evanston: Northwestern UP, 1990.

——. *Painterly Abstraction in Modernist American Poetry*. Cambridge: Cambridge UP, 1989.

——. 'Spectacular Anti-Spectacle: Ecstasy and Nationality in Whitman and his Heirs'. Lecture. European Association of American Studies Conference. U of Lisbon, April 1998.

Anderson, Benedict. *Imagined Communities: Reflections on the Origin and Spread of Nationalism*. London: Verso, 1983.

Barrell, John. *The Dark Side of the Landscape*. Cambridge: Cambridge UP, 1980.

Bates, Milton J. *Wallace Stevens: A Mythology of Self*. Berkeley: U of California P, 1985.

Berger, Charles. *Forms of Farewell: The Late Poetry of Wallace Stevens*. Madison: U of Wisconsin P, 1985.

Beyers, Chris. 'Stevens and Ludwig Richter'. *Wallace Stevens Journal* 18.2 (Fall 1994): 197–206.

Bloom, Harold. *Wallace Stevens: The Poems of Our Climate*. Ithaca: Cornell UP, 1977.

——. *The Western Canon: The Books and the School of the Ages*. New York: Harcourt Brace, 1994.

Bové, Paul. *Destructive Poetics: Heidegger and Modern American Poetry*. New York: Columbia UP, 1980.

Brazeau, Peter. *Parts of a World: Wallace Stevens Remembered: An Oral Biography*. San Francisco: North Point P, 1985.

Bryant, William Cullen. *Picturesque America*. 8 vols. New York. 1872–74.

——. *Poems of William Cullen Bryant*. Oxford: Oxford UP, 1914.

Carpenter, Frederick. *Robinson Jeffers*. New York: Grosset & Dunlap, 1962.

Carroll, Joseph. *Wallace Stevens' Supreme Fiction: A New Romanticism*. Baton Rouge LA: Lousiana State UP, 1987.

Carson, Ciaran. 'Escaped from the Massacre?' Rev. of *North*, by Seamus Heaney. *Honest Ulsterman* 50 (Winter 1975): 184–5.

Chernyshevsky, Nikolay Gavrilovich. *What Is to Be Done?* [*Chto delat?*]. 1863. Trans. Michael R. Katz. Ithaca: Cornell UP, 1989.

Coleridge, Samuel Taylor. *Biographia Literaria*. 1817; London: Everyman, 1975.

Cook, Eleanor. *Against Coercion: Games Poets Play.* Stanford: Stanford UP, 1998.

Cooper, James Fenimore. *The Pioneers.* 1823; Oxford: Oxford UP, 1991.

Costello, Bonnie. 'Effects of an Analogy: Wallace Stevens and Painting'. *Wallace Stevens: The Poetics of Modernism.* Ed. Albert Gelpi. Cambridge: Cambridge UP, 1985. 65–85.

——. 'Wallace Stevens: The Adequacy of Landscape'. *Wallace Stevens Journal* 17.2 (Fall 1993): 203–18.

Coyle, Beverly and Alan Filreis, eds. *Secretaries of the Moon: The Letters of Wallace Stevens and José Rodríguez Feo.* Durham: Duke UP, 1986.

Dickinson, Emily. *The Poems of Emily Dickinson.* 3 vols. Ed. Thomas H. Johnson. Cambridge, MA: Belknap–Harvard UP, 1955.

Doggett, Frank. *Stevens' Poetry of Thought.* Baltimore: Johns Hopkins UP, 1966.

DuRose, Lisa. 'Racial Domain and the Imagination of Wallace Stevens'. *Wallace Stevens Journal* 22.1 (Spring 1998): 3–22.

Eliot, T. S. *After Strange Gods: A Primer of Modern Heresy.* London: Faber & Faber, 1934.

Emerson, Ralph Waldo. *Selected Writings of Emerson.* Ed. Donald McQuade. New York: Modern Library, 1981.

Filreis, Alan. *Modernism from Right to Left: Wallace Stevens, the Thirties, and Literary Radicalism.* Cambridge: Cambridge UP, 1994.

——. *Wallace Stevens and the Actual World.* Princeton: Princeton UP, 1991.

Fitter, Chris. *Poetry, Space, Landscape.* Cambridge: Cambridge UP, 1995.

Fitzgerald, F. Scott. *The Great Gatsby.* 1926; Harmondsworth: Penguin, 1986.

Frost, Robert. *The Poetry of Robert Frost.* Ed. Edward Connery Lathem. London: Cape, 1972.

Graham, Jorie. *The End of Beauty.* Hopewell, NJ: Ecco, 1987.

——. *The Errancy.* Hopewell, NJ: Ecco, 1997.

Halliday, Mark. *Stevens and the Interpersonal.* Princeton: Princeton UP, 1991.

Hardy, Thomas. *Far From the Madding Crowd.* 1874; London: Macmillan, 1922.

Harvey, David. *Justice, Nature and the Geography of Difference.* Oxford: Blackwell, 1996.

Heaney, Seamus. *North.* London: Faber & Faber, 1975.

Hecht, Anthony. *On the Laws of the Poetic Art.* Princeton: Princeton UP, 1995.

Helsinger, Elizabeth. 'Turner and the Representation of England'. *Landscape and Power.* Ed. W. J. T. Mitchell. Chicago: U of Chicago P, 1994. 103–25.

Hertz, David Michael. *Angels of Reality: Emersonian Unfoldings in Wright, Stevens, and Ives.* Carbondale: Southern Illinois UP, 1993.

Jameson, Fredric. 'Wallace Stevens'. *New Orleans Review* 11 (1984): 10–19. Rpt in *Critical Essays on Wallace Stevens.* Eds Stephen Gould Axelrod and Helen Deese. Boston: G. K. Hall, 1988. 171–96.

Jarrell, Randall. *Poetry and the Age.* 1953; New York: Farrar, 1972.

Jeffers, Robinson. *Selected Poems.* New York: Vintage, 1965.

——. *The Selected Poetry of Robinson Jeffers.* New York: Random, 1959.

Kazin, Alfred. *On Native Grounds: An Interpretation of Modern American Prose.* 1942; New York: Doubleday, 1956.

Kermode, Frank. *The Sense of an Ending: Studies in the Theory of Fiction.* Oxford: Oxford UP, 1968.

Lefebvre, Henri. *The Production of Space.* Trans. Donald Nicholson-Smith. Oxford: Blackwell, 1992.

Lentricchia, Frank. *After the New Criticism*. London: Methuen, 1983.

——. *Ariel and the Police*. Brighton: Harvester, 1988.

——. *Modernist Quartet*. Cambridge: Cambridge UP, 1994.

Lindemann, Gottfried. *History of German Art: Painting Sculpture Architecture*. Trans. Tessa Sayle. London: Pall Mall, 1971.

Lombardi, Thomas Francis. *Wallace Stevens and the Pennsylvania Keystone*. Selinsgrove: Susquehanna UP, 1996.

Longenbach, James. *Wallace Stevens: The Plain Sense of Things*. New York: Oxford UP, 1991.

McGann, Jerome. *Black Riders: The Visible Language of Modernism*. Princeton: Princeton UP, 1993.

——. *The Romantic Ideology: A Critical Investigation*. Chicago: U of Chicago P, 1983.

MacLeod, Glen. *Wallace Stevens and Modern Art*. New Haven, CT: Yale UP, 1993.

Matterson, Stephen. Letter to the author. 26 Aug. 1995.

Matthiessen, F. O. 'Society and Solitude'. Rev. of *Ideas of Order*, by Wallace Stevens. *Yale Review* 25. 3 (Mar. 1936): 605–7.

Miller, J. Hillis. 'Stevens' Rock and Criticism as Cure.' Parts I, II. *Georgia Review* 30 (1976): 5–31; 330–48.

Milton, John. *Complete Shorter Poems*. Ed. John Carey. London: Longman, 1981.

Miskinis, Steven. 'Exceeding Responsibilities: Politics, History, and the Hero in Wallace Stevens' War Poetry'. *Wallace Stevens Journal* 20.2 (Fall 1996): 209–28.

Mitchell, W. J. T. 'Imperial Landscape'. *Landscape and Power*. Ed. W. J. T. Mitchell. Chicago: U of Chicago P, 1994. 5–34.

——. Introduction. *Landscape and Power*. Ed. W. J. T. Mitchell. Chicago: U of Chicago P, 1994. 1–4.

Morrison, Toni. *Playing in the Dark: Whiteness and the Literary Imagination*. London: Picador, 1993.

Moynihan, Robert. 'Checklist: Second Purchase, Wallace Stevens Collection, Huntington Library'. *Wallace Stevens Journal* 20.1 (Spring 1996): 76–103.

Nabokov, Vladimir. *The Annotated Lolita*. Revd ed. Ed. Alfred Appel Jr. London: Weidenfeld & Nicolson, 1993.

Nietzsche, Friedrich. *The Birth of Tragedy* and *The Case of Wagner*. Trans. Walter Kaufmann. New York: Vintage, 1967.

O'Hara, Daniel T. 'Imaginary Politics: Emerson, Stevens and the Resistance of Style'. *Wallace Stevens and the Feminine*. Ed. Melita Schaum. Tuscaloosa: U of Alabama P, 1993.

Patke, Rajeev S. *The Long Poems of Wallace Stevens*. Cambridge: Cambridge UP, 1985.

Pearce, Roy Harvey. *The Continuity of American Poetry*. 3rd ed. Princeton: Princeton UP, 1965.

Perlis, Alan. *Wallace Stevens: A World of Transforming Shapes*. London: Associated UPs, 1976.

Perloff, Marjorie. 'Revolving in Crystal: The Supreme Fiction and the Impasse of the Modernist Lyric'. *Wallace Stevens: The Poetics of Modernism*. Ed. Albert Gelpi. Cambridge: Cambridge UP, 1985. 41–64.

Poirier, Richard. *Robert Frost: The Work of Knowing*. New York: Oxford UP, 1977.

——. *A World Elsewhere*. New York: Oxford UP, 1966.

Rich, Adrienne. *What Is Found There: Notebooks on Poetry and Politics*. New York: Norton, 1995.

Richards, I. A. *Coleridge on Imagination*. London: Kegan Paul, 1934.

Richardson, Joan. *Wallace Stevens: The Early Years, 1879–1923.* New York: William Morrow, 1986.

——. *Wallace Stevens: The Later Years, 1923–1955.* New York: William Morrow, 1988.

Riddel, Joseph N. *The Clairvoyant Eye: the Poetry and Poetics of Wallace Stevens.* Baton Rouge: Louisiana UP, 1965.

Rilke, Rainer Maria. *The Selected Poetry of Rainer Maria Rilke.* Trans. Stephen Mitchell New York: Vintage, 1989.

Rowe, John Carlos. *At Emerson's Tomb: The Politics of Classic American Literature.* New York: Columbia UP, 1997.

Safranski, Rüdiger. *Martin Heidegger: Between Good and Evil.* Trans. Ewald Osers. Cambridge, MA: Harvard UP, 1998.

Schaum, Melita, *Wallace Stevens and the Critical Schools.* Tuscaloosa: U of Alabama P, 1988.

——, ed. *Wallace Stevens and the Feminine.* Tuscaloosa: U of Alabama P, 1993

Shenton, Donald R. Untitled. Wallace Stevens Memorial Issue. *The Historical Review of Berks County* 24.4 (Fall 1959): 108.

Sperry, Stuart M. 'Wallace Stevens and the Seasons'. *Southern Review* 33. 3 (Summer 1997): 605–27.

Spiegelman, Willard. *Majestic Indolence: English Romantic Poetry and the Work of Art.* Oxford: Oxford UP, 1995.

Stevens, Wallace. *Sur Plusieurs Beaux Sujets.* Ed. Milton J. Bates. Stanford: Stanford UP, 1989.

Vendler, Helen. *The Art of Shakespeare's Sonnets.* Cambridge, MA: Belknap–Harvard UP, 1997.

——. *Words Chosen Out of Desire.* Cambridge, MA: Harvard UP, 1986.

——. *On Extended Wings: Wallace Stevens' Longer Poems.* Cambridge, MA: Harvard UP, 1969.

Voros, Gyorgyi. *Notations of the Wild: Ecology in the Poetry of Wallace Stevens.* Iowa City: U of Iowa P, 1997.

Williams, William Carlos. *Paterson.* Ed. Christopher MacGowan. Revd ed. Manchester: Carcanet, 1992.

Wilson, Rob. *American Sublime: The Genealogy of a Poetic Genre.* Madison: U of Wisconsin P, 1991.

Wordsworth, William. *The Prelude: A Parallel Text.* Ed. J. C. Maxwell. Harmondsworth: Penguin, 1986.

Zawacki, Andrew. Letter to the author. 9 Mar. 1998.

Index of works by Wallace Stevens

General index

Roney, Lila James 137
Rossi, Mario 35
Rowe, John Carlos 79, 145n.
Ruisdael, Jacob 109

Sandburg, Carl 30, 84
Saturday Evening Post 72
Schaum, Melita 2
Schopenhauer, Alfred 138
Schuylkill River, PA 117, 131–3
Serge, Victor 51, 55, 60
Shenton, Donald R. 117
Sibelius, Jan 124
Simons, Hi 3, 35, 113
Sophocles 103
Smetana, Bedřich 124
Sperry, Stuart M. 142
Spiegelman, Willard 63
Stevens, Elsie Moll 122
Stevens, Holly 113, 117
Stevens, Wallace
    and art 11, 32–4, 49–50, 56–7, 107–8
    and critical theory 38–9, 43, 62, 79–80
    and criticism 1980–97 3, 9–12
    and Holly Stevens (daughter) 113
    and Garrett Barcalow Stevens (father)
        79
    and genealogy 75, 79–80, 91, 111–21, 137
    and landscape painting 49–51, 56–7
    and racism 4, 79, 131, 139–42
    and Romanticism 3–5, 9, 27, 35, 38, 60,
        62–3, 94–5, 105, 122–3

and tragedy 76–7, 79, 85, 103
and USA/nationalism 79–81, 92–3,
    97–9, 111, 124–5, 137

Thoreau, Henry David 130
Tinicum, PA 112
Tomlinson, Charles 119
Toulet, Paul-Jean 59–60
Truman, Harry 86
Tulpehocken, PA 112, 117
Turner, William 39
Twain, Mark 121

Valéry, Paul 89
van Geyzel, Leonard C. 7–8, 14, 22–3, 123,
    125, 129, 147n.
Vendler, Helen 10, 73, 101, 106, 145–6n.
von Schwind, Moritz 49
Voros, Gyorgyi 15, 36

Watteau, Antoine 11
Whitman, Walt 19, 44, 80, 92, 112, 124
Whittier, John Greenleaf 135
Williams, William Carlos 96, 99
Wilson, Rob 3, 142
Wordsworth, William 27, 62–3, 94, 105,
    122

Yeats, W. B. 68, 112, 124

Zawacki, Andrew 145n
Zeller, John 116, 120